Insights of a *Poet's Soul...*

Views and Thoughts...The Way I See It

by Jessica Michelle

DORRANCE
PUBLISHING CO
EST. 1920
PITTSBURGH, PENNSYLVANIA 15238

Dorrance Publishing Co
585 Alpha Drive
Suite 103
Pittsburgh, PA 15238
Visit our website at *www.dorrancebookstore.com*

ISBN: 978-1-6376-4177-4
eISBN: 978-1-6376-4813-1

Insights of a Poet's Soul...

VIEWS AND THOUGHTS...THE WAY I SEE IT

Dedication

It will take a lifetime to truly thank everyone who had a part in the making of this book. However, I'm going to try to sum it up in a few words.

Without God, there would be nothing. I thank him and give him all the glory. I'm using the very gift he has given me.

To my children. Every time I look in their eyes, I know that I have to teach them that anything is possible. I thank them for pushing me.

To my family and friends, and the ones who said that I would never make it. To those who endured my practice notes, poems, and dictations.

And to you…the reader. It's rare in this day and age to get a young person to put down the remote or phone and pick up a book. So I'm thanking you, my readers, who appreciate the fine art of poetry.

Enjoy this book, because I enjoyed writing it.

My Apology…

Okay, readers, this book has explicit language. If you're not old enough to read this…please put it down. I held back with the first book, but I feel now you guys have a sense about me and my writing. So I let my hair down (so to speak).

So don't get offended by this book. I love words and am a firm believer of freedom of speech and press. Prepare yourself before you start, because believe me, you're not going to want to put this down.

Words From The Author...

HELLO AGAIN! Just let me tell you how completing my third book made me feel. I had so many mixed emotions as I was typing it out. Some of you may not know this, but that book was twenty years in the making.

I realized that I went through all those trials and tribulations so I can become the person I am today. All the people that came in and out of my life were actually put there for reasons. I've learned something from each and every one of them and wrote some of the best poems that I have ever written.

I don't regret going through anything in my life. I don't regret letting people that I knew were bad influences or underhanded in my life.

I now know that the heartache, pain, and all the tears I shed were all worth it. Remember, what doesn't kill us makes us stronger. That's one thing that I always tell people when they ask, "Why did you stay with that person?" or "How could you let that person in your life?" I believe everything that we go through in life is a life lesson. And you never stop learning. It's just how you deal with what divides us all.

My way of handling it is through writing. I write about everything. If I'm hurt, I pick up the pen. If I'm crying, my notebook or Blackberry is in my hands. Some of my best work has come from some of my darkest days.

So with that being said, I hope you enjoy my third book as much my earlier ones.

Escaping Reality...

It seems to appear to be
That addiction is one's way of escaping reality
For a while to become someone looking in
Instead of being the center of it all
Why not take something to ease the pain when one falls
Lapsing through a moment when you see
What is not really seen
To have that defining moment when you think
That it was all a dream
Who wouldn't want to escape the hardship
Of what this world and what life brings
And really answer the question
Who gives a fuck why the caged bird sings
Forget how it feels
To bottle one's fears and indifference
And all the worries and blame
Put on by someone else's shit, not to mention
So why not hit it once, knock back a couple
Pop a pill or two
'Cause who wants to continue to face
A fucked-up reality when the only bitch who falls...is you

Thoughts Of My Life...

My moment of darkness when I'm afraid to close my eyes at night
Frightened by the images and thoughts that cloud my mind and sight
Darkness has a way of bringing demons to light
And the Devil stays on me no matter how hard I fight
I try to close my eyes and envision a much more sensible way to live
But settling for less than I deserve is too high of a price to give
Why live less than you should to help bring happiness to someone…who isn't you
Putting their emotions and feelings before you even think about you
Life is too short and getting shorter by the day
Why be the creator of your own unhappiness…why stand in your own way
Stepping on the stones of life is expected on the road less traveled
But being the stones that people step on is way too much for my mind to fathom
Separate church from state is easier if you were a politician
But damn, it gets a little complex if you don't have a pot to piss in
Relying on one's judgment when it's clouded by the weight of the world
With all the growing up I did only to realize I'm still that scared young girl
Who said that the rain doesn't last always and that there's a silver lining in each cloud
Man, were they wrong, my cloud didn't get that memo, because it hasn't stop pouring down
On my own existence on every step that I take
The burden of life has taken a toll on my mind, my body, my soul is about to break
So say what you want, say what you will
These are my thoughts and opinions, who gives a fuck how you feel

Love No More...

Try to turn the world against me
And have them all question you
Keep trying to deceive me
And think nothing's gonna happen to you
You've cried wolf too many times
For anyone to ever trust or believe you
Try to fit me as a worthless parent
And now all the jokes are on you
I've learned in life that sacrifices must be made
To rid yourself of the wrong path that was laid
I chose to go left when everything inside cried right
Now this shit I live with is nothing but fuss and fight
I let my past interrupt my future, which fucked up my life
Someone should have told me that love don't last,
now I'm stuck being your wife
I've let go…but you…you hold on
The flame has been out, now it's time for your ass to be gone
Nothing will ever make me love you no matter how hard you try
My heart has grown hard to those fake-ass tears you cry
Where there's no air nothing can live
If you don't stop with the abuse and mind games
I don't know how I can forget and forgive
I don't know if you get what I'm trying to say
If not let me spell it out for you…go on your merry way
'Cause love don't live here anymore and neither do I
So love me in your dreams as you continue to cry

Not Another Love Poem...

There's nothing left to say but goodbye
Wiping the tears away from your cheek as we cry
To feel like we will never see each other another day
No more long walks, warm kisses, seeing each other's face
Just a phone call, a plane ride away
It will only last a couple of weeks before we go our separate ways
It is better than to be loved than to have never loved at all
But whose heart will feel like a ton of bricks when no one answers that call
If it makes you happy then just walk away
I don't want you to choose but I'd really like it if you stay
Let's bring our dream of us together a reality
Because you truly are the only one for me

Clever Nasty...

I whisper in your ear
Those unforgettable nothings you want to hear
I touch you in the places where I should only go
Have you make that noise that no one has ever heard before
Starting at your feet to those unbelievable thighs
Watching those faces you make as I look in those beautiful eyes
Opening your legs wider as my hands and mouth begin to play
Licking you ever so softly because there's no other way
Kissing the mouth that never speaks a word
As my hands slowly grasp upward
Making my way to your belly, palming the small of your back
Hearing that soft moan lets me know you like it like that
Your breasts are so soft and tender to the touch
Clawing my back in ecstasy as I begin to thrust
No oils, no lotion, no synthetic lubricant is needed
Having your body shaking and trembling and my job is yet to be completed
I didn't know you were flexible, how'd you get your leg like that
Turning you over so I can invade you from the back
Pushing me off you as you get on top and proceed to ride
Hitting all the spots that sometimes are hard to find
And just before our merry-go-round is just about through
You hop off and start sucking and licking 'cause you like to swallow the juice

Not Mine...

Falling in love with what we do
Upset because I'm not who you're going home to
The way you touch my body making me want more
Leaving me in pure ecstasy when you walk out my door
Side bitch, next bitch, call me what you like
If that bitch was doing her job you wouldn't be here tonight

Sometimes I don't wanna close my eyes
Imagination so strong I still feel you fisting between my thighs
Bodies thrusting, blood rushing through my vines
Moaning and trying to not call the Lord's name in vain
Don't want this to end, keep playing with her like that
See if you can make her cry when you hit from the back

Phone's ringing, is that yours or mine
Your girl can wait while you invading me from behind
Pulling my hair, choking me a bit
Trying not to gag on your enormous dick
Slap it, Daddy, all this is yours, it has your name on it
Grocery shopping and killing it, put my name on your list

Wannabe...

Ol' pussy-ass soft-ass nigga
Wannabe muthafuckin' baller
Don't have two cents to rub together
Have to use your boy phone just to call her
Ain't shit, ain't never gonna be shit
Trying to hide the little boy you are
But every time you show your face that pussy nigga's not far
Think you bad 'cause bitches be jocking you
They're attracted to bullshit-ass niggas and that would be you
Money over bitches is what you live by
You probably would have both if your stupid ass wasn't always getting high
You're lost, you needed someone like me on your team
But keep fucking with that bitch, you'll see her true color...green
Not like money, she don't got that green
That bitch will lock you up...if you know what I mean

How Much Is Too Much...

When will it be too much for you to just give up
Say fuck the world 'cause you feel that you're stuck
People running over you, treating you as a doormat
When will it be too much for you to say FUCK that

When will the wrong person say the wrong thing at the wrong time
Wake up and grab a piece of your own mind
Stop giving other people the power over you
When will it be too much for you to have control over you

When will it be too much for you to quit saying "yes" and learn to say "no"
Tell them they've worn out their welcome and it's time to go
How much is too much, will you ever figure it out

Thinking Out Loud...

They say if you don't stand for something you will fall for anything. In life there are plenty of things you should stand for. One is yourself, you need to be your biggest fan. If you don't believe in yourself, who do you expect to believe in you? Never feel that you can't do something because of the obstacles. Because it's too time consuming or it's hard. Nothing in life is easy, if you want something bad enough you would do anything to get it. Yeah, there may be people who don't think you can do it, but how low will they feel when you come out on top? Any accomplishment no matter how big or small should be celebrated. Don't belittle yourself because of simpleminded, egotistical people, who don't see the brilliant person you are, and the great person you're going to be. Another is your family, you are a big impact on your family. There are people who have your back. Even estranged families have concerns about your wellbeing. Never turn your back on them no matter what disagreements you may have had. Don't burn your bridge, you'll never know if you need to cross it again. Lastly, but should've been first, God. When you're going through hardship and you think he's turned his back on you, he didn't. He just wants to see how much you believe in him. Is your faith strong enough to aide you through hard times? He loves you unconditionally even when you don't love yourself. He will never put anything on you that you can't bear. The words I've said are just thoughts, I've written down. Someone out there needed to hear and/or read them. If I relieved someone's thoughts and stress I've done what I set off to do. Life is too short, always be a believer in you. Only you stand in your way to success.

Think About It...

Where can you go to free your mind of all your worries?
To hide away from despair and pain
To open yourself to yourself and discuss the direction your life is going
Where can you go to get away from everyone else's problems
To set aside the stress and frustration of everything on your shoulders
Step back and stop living their lives for them
If you go where you could go, do you think anyone would know
Do you think that they would take ownership,
take care of their own responsibilities
Think about it
If you weren't who you are who would they go to
And if you were where they are who would help you
Think about it

Why Not Me...

I'm not too tall, not too short, I'm somewhere in between
I'm not too thin, not too fat, my ass looks good in jeans
I'm not a ten, not a five, I say I'm about an eight
You can ask the men I've been with, they say the sex is great
You say you want a chick who's always by your side
We could be like Bonnie and Clyde 'cause I'm always down to ride
I could be that lady in the streets and that freak you want in bed
I'm telling you I'm what you want, I got that fire-ass head
It could be one night, I'm not asking you for life
I'm just in it for sex, I'm already another man's wife
But I could drop him if you want me to yourself
I got skills to get it up, I really don't need any outside unwanted help
They say two is company, three's a crowd
But I say add another chick and I'll show you how I get down
You don't have to prove yourself to me, I already know what you got
I love when you go down on me, you always hit that spot
You can call me nasty, you can call me naughty, call me what you like
As long as you're saying it while you're laying that pipe
If not all of you then part of you, I'll take what I can get
Just thinking about you next to me always get me wet

Well Played, Sir...

You made me fall in love with you
Doing all the amazing things you do
Then you dropped me like a bad habit
Now I'm feening 'cause I can't have it
Well played, Sir

Looking at me from across the room
Knowing that the end is coming soon
Motioning that you want to get down
To only make me feel like a clown
Well played, Sir

Having her pick up the phone when I called you
Not being man enough to tell me we're though
Knowing all along how I felt about you
Damn, I hate I'm in love with you
Well played, Sir

I'm gonna do unto you as you did unto me
So to hell with you, you've been set free
My heart is numb, my mind is clear
So fuck you, I'm outta here
Well played...Ma'am

Happy New Year...

You say write my thoughts down on paper so I can see what went wrong
But all I see is garbage, what the hell is going on
Don't want the New Year to end up like the last
So I try to put all that stress and drama where it belongs…in the past

First day of the year and I wake up feeling the same
Starting to believe that nothing's really ever gonna change
Same ol' same shitty job, nowhere to go
I feel like picking up and leaving, go for what I know

Maybe a different location will leave behind everything I'm trying to avoid
All this shit around me, I easily get annoyed
But till then I'll play it by ear
Oh, I almost forgot…Happy Fucking New Year

When The Wind Blows...

When the wind blows you can hear a quiet whisper
You can see the leaves dancing among themselves
Baby birds fly, feeling the wind in their wings
Squirrels playing hide-and-seek with their nut

When the wind blows there's a cool, refreshing breeze
Kids playing double-Dutch and hopscotch
Laughter roaring from miles and miles
Picking up pick-up sticks while the wind wipes away tears of joy
When the wind blows it gives chills to the little ones in the pool
Helping the people in the heat cool down
Aiding kites to glide higher and higher
Happiness comes when the wind blows

But what happens when the wind blows so hard and so rough
Strong enough to blow away cars and tear down houses
Leaving bodies of innocent bystanders
What happens when the mighty wind couples with the mighty rain?
When it's so devastating we give them names
Remember Andrew, Katrina, and Fay
People, loved ones we lost due to Mother Nature
Just Remember...

Obama...

Home of the brave, land of the free
Why is this world killing people like you and me
Loving oneself and loving one's country go hand and hand
Who started this war, oh, one little simple-minded man
Like father like son, everybody say, I guess that saying must be true
Just like Papa Bush, Lil' Bush wants to start a war too
But how many more people must die so he can see whose "war" is bigger
Now he's saying let's pull our troops out before they elect this nigger
So they can say he was a good president,
he did what he did for the good of the people
Let the families of the ones who died stand before him so he can meet them
Children growing up with no moms or dads
Mothers losing the only child they had
Lives being turned upside down, twisted in so many ways
Everyone's holding their breath to see if he has something intelligent to say
No, nothing, just the same old lies
Isn't he the lucky one, he doesn't come home to children's cries
Now is a time of change
Let's back someone with a different last name
Someone who knows the value of his people's worth
He didn't pick Hillary, some people think that was a mistake
But how can we change if we still have an ex-president who has a hand in
the decisions his wife makes
Don't get me wrong, Clinton was damn near the best
But let's see what Obama can do, let's put him to the test
What he plans to do a lot of people agree
Medicare, education, poverty, and equality mean a lot to me
How can people say he's going to bring upon another great depression
That's mostly rich people who are afraid that someone wants to help us
Every person wants to feel like there's someone looking out for them
I back Obama because I want change just like him

15

A Dream Within A Dream...

What if we're living inside one man's dream
That the life we know is not what it seems
Poverty and devastation is not really real
And the hurt and pain is not what we feel
What if this man wakes up one day
Will all of our lives and hard work all fade away
Everything we went through was just a game
What if this one guy had no name
Are we amusing him with each passing of every day
And if he could talk to us what would he say
Do you think he would guide us on what to do
I would love some help, wouldn't you
Maybe life isn't so hard, maybe we're getting in our own way
If this isn't some man's dream and you had a choice, would you want to stay
If poverty, devastation, heartaches, and pain was real
Would you be here going through what you don't want to go through still
What if this is a dream inside a dream within this one man's dream
Can you imagine the things we've done, the things he's seen
What if we can't explain the way we choose to live our lives
And the shame is so strong we can't stand to look him in his eyes

Dear Me...

What happened to that girl who was always so sure of herself
Didn't let anyone get to her and put all the things
She didn't want to deal with on a shelf
Who was kindhearted and put everyone before her
Would take the shirt off her back if they needed it from her
Oh my God, did she wake up one day
and say I'm tired of people walking over me
Damn, it's about time you finally opened your eyes to see
Trust is something earned, not given away
You were too trusting, wanting too many unhealthy things to stay
Who needed friends, you were great alone
Now those friends got you in a place you don't belong
When you split with your husband what did you think you would find
You can't find happiness if you're not in the right state of mind
You got yourself in shit you never thought you'd be in
Now trying to drown your problems in a gallon of gin
To each its own, for you it's worse
I believe you forgot to put God first

Imperfection...

You make me want to be a better me
You see things in me that I wish I could see
We sit and say nothing sometimes
But it seems like you know everything that's on my mind
My self-esteem has always been through the roof
But there are times I doubt my ability and youth
My looks are fading and thin is a thing of the past
But the way you look at me, I just want that feeling to last
You see through my flaws and all my imperfections
And give me all your love, your heart, and your affection

Great Romance...

My knight in shining armor
The one who got through
Every time I close my eyes
I see and feel you
The way you touch me, the way I felt
I promise every time you looked at me
My heart would melt
I opened up my heart and let you in
And that is how this great romance began
Always together, never apart
I thought we'd always be one
Right from the start
One last kiss from you
One last rumble
Now I know what they meant by my heart
You fumbled
It's hard to say goodbye to you
I never thought I would
My love for you will never end
My heart will always be true
I found love when you entered my life
So for that I will always love you

Random Thought...

Will the real men please step up
Show these little boys how to treat a queen
Shower them with love, embrace their soul, mind, heart,
just not what's in between
Talk is cheap and so is the game you're trying to spit
This is the time I wish I had one so I can say suck my dick

Just More Thoughts...

Love, WTF is love. A wasted emotion. The energy it takes for a person to find someone and fall in love could be used for something more practical. People blame love on everything, they treat it like a "get out of jail free" card. I hit you because I love you. Really? Because if that's love believe me, I can do without it. The things people do and put up with just to hear those words spoken by another person is fucking ridiculous. Who said that life is not worth living alone? Shit, give me a dog, a cat, something, I really don't need any added stress. Why should I open my heart over and over again if the outcome is simply going to be the same? People go crazy if others don't return the same love they feel as though they are giving. People actually kill people because they say that they loved them so much that they don't want to see them with anyone else. That's crazy!!! I would rather be by myself, fuck trying to be loved. I love myself so much that there isn't any room for anyone else to love me. At least that way I won't have to die over the name of love. People have given love a bad name. Do they not know that's not love, that's obsession? If you don't know the meaning of the word it could look the same. I think that I could live the rest of my life not being in love with another human being. What's wrong with just calling someone when you need companionship? They're so many mechanicals boyfriends out there where I don't have to worry about getting a disease. Fuck love, don't need it, don't want it, it's just heartache waiting to happen.

Again, just my thoughts…

Too Real...

Empty my heart as well as my mind
Release my thoughts and there you will find
Here lies unhappiness and here lies grief
I'll tell you my life story and I'll try to be brief
Looking out a window, a mirror of my vitality
Searching for something else other than reality
Glancing under objects that are lying in the road
Hoping to get a glimpse of that story that's always told
A moment in time when the seasons lie still
A numbness in my soul is the only thing I feel
As I close my eyes my memories become clear
And I realize there's so much to fear
Like growing old and hopelessly alone
The only bright spot in my life would be when my kids decide to visit home
Or blowing everything and having to start at square one
And notice that the end of my life has just begun
Even better, having the love of my life walking out on me on that special day
Looking upon family and friends speechless, searching for words to say
Then I open my eyes and realize that I'm in the corner of my wall
Trying to grab ahold of something, so I don't fall
The time and energy it took for me to think of those things
Could've been spent doing something positive
with the hope of what the future may bring
See, some people are like that, only think of all the bad moments that occur in time
Always stressed out, on the verge of a breakdown
But when you ask them how they're doing—it's always fine
It helps to take time from the madness of this world to find yourself
Because if you continue down the road you're on you'll see that every-
thing's gone—that there's nothing left

22

I'm Always Thinking...

In life people's paths cross. It's no coincidence that I met you. There was no way to know the effect you would have on me. When I have a bad day, you're the first person I think to call. On a good day you're the reason for it all. My thoughts are racing, every time I see your face. My body is yearning to feel your warm embrace. You teach me every day the secrets of life. I'm yours, you're mine, no need to think twice.

In life we get caught up in our own bullshit. Forgetting about the ones who care for us. And who would move the world if they could. The ones who don't ask for much, just love in return. Why is it that others aren't happy unless you're miserable? Why is it that they know the one thing that could fuck up your day? Pass it off like it's a joke they were jk'ing. Life's not a game, emotions are golden.

What point is it to see someone depressed, what joy do you get out of it? To truly love someone you must see the world through their eyes. It is the most unselfish act, to let go. To make another person happy. Things will never be the same, just let go and let it be. Release me for your grasp, and let me be free. I feel as though I'm suffocating under your wings. I can now associate with why the caged bird sings.

Do you think the only way to talk to me is to argue? The stress and emotional drain you take me through, is the reason I fell out of love with you. Nothing feels the same when it's just us two. Why don't we build a bridge over it and drive right through? Why prolong the inevitable, this was never supposed to last. Stayed together for the kids, now I'm stuck with your ass. Always saying things will get better, how you're gonna change. If so why do we always end up at this same place? Care to explain? You're right, I'm wrong, let's agree to disagree. I'm seeing another side of myself and I don't like what I see.

So these are just my thoughts, something written to clear my mind. Seeking the perfect life, the one I'm trying to find. I don't know what is going to make me happy. But trust, this is not what it is. I think I left my heart in New York. Maybe I need a trip to find the Wiz.

Just As Friends...

A slight brush on the lips, a warm hand on mine
A soft whisper in my ear and I'm thinking it's about time
For us just as friends isn't going to work out
Because it's you I want in my life without a doubt
Anxiety I feel when I see your face each day
Waiting for you to change your mind and see things my way
One night of passion is all I need to sway your mind
To make you forget about everyone else and only have me on your mind
As you caress my body gently with my warm breast in your hands
Mesmerized by my beauty, having you move on demand
See, that's why we just can't be friends
Because I would have to wake up and my dream would have to end

Betrayed...

I thought you were my friend
Remember, best friends till the end
Who knew the end would be today
As I see you and my man together in my bed as y'all lay
I took you in when everyone else turned you away
I was the only one there when you needed a place to stay
You know me better than I knew myself
If you don't leave right now you're gonna need some help
I can't believe you, we were like sisters too
How could you put our friendship in jeopardy? How could you
I told you things I wouldn't think about telling anyone else
Don't try to explain to me, keep that shit to yourself
I blame myself, I saw the way you two act
Always laughing and whispering every time I turned my back
Oh, but it didn't start with him, this began a long time ago
Remember my baby daddy, oh, you thought I didn't know
I don't want to hear friends are forever, niggas come and go
True friends just don't let that shit happen, you know
I knew those weren't my panties underneath my bed
And he was saying it was all in my head

But now I'm tired of talking, I'm finished with the both of you
Go ahead, take her to Motel 6 and finish doing what you do
Don't worry, your things will be on the curb waiting for you
So pick them up on the way back when you're through
Don't try to call me, my number will be changed
How about you just forget you even know my name
I can do bad by myself with no help from you
So keep your distance if you know what's best for you

So back to me randomly speaking on behalf of love. Again, these are just my thoughts on this particular day.

Love, what the fuck is love? A wasted emotion, the energy it takes for a person to fall in love could be used for something more practical. People blame love for everything. They treat it like a "get out of jail free" card. "I hit you because I love you." Really, because if that's love believe me, I can do without it.

The things people do just to hear those words spoken by another person, it's damn ridiculous. Who said that life is not worth living alone? Shit, give me a dog or a cat any day. I really don't need the added stress. Why should I open my heart over and over again, if the outcome is simply going to be the same?

People go crazy if others don't return the same love they feel as though they are giving. Seriously, they actually kill others because they say that they love them so much that they don't want to see them with anyone else. That's crazy! I would rather be by myself, fuck trying to be loved. I love myself so much that there isn't any room for anyone else to love me. At least that way I won't have to die for the name of love. People have given love a bad name. Do they not know that's not love but obsession? If you don't know the meaning of the word it could look the same.

I think that I could live the rest of my life not being in love with another human being. What's wrong with just calling someone when you feel the need for companionship?

So some of my poems don't have titles. Not that I couldn't come up with any, but because I felt like you guys might interpret them and find that they don't pertain to just one subject sometimes. I hope you guys enjoyed what you've read so far. Fasten your seatbelts and prepare for my literary orgasms.

My knight in silver armor
The one who got through
Every time I close my eyes
I see and feel you
The way you touch me, the way I felt
I promise every time you looked at me my heart would just melt
I opened up my heart to you and let you in
And that is how this great romance began
Always together, never apart
I thought we'd always be one right from the start
One last kiss from you, one last rumble
Now I know how it feels when they say my heart you fumbled
It's hard to say goodbye to you, I never thought I would
My love for you will never end, my heart will always be true
I found love when you entered my life so far that I will always love you
What was I thinking to even start again?
Just jumping into a relationship, not even starting as friends
I know I can't be the one and only and I hate feeling like I'm last
But when we come together that this uneasiness would just pass

It's not fair for us to continue going

Not just for us but for the unknowing

It's not fair that I ask for time you don't possess

And I get mad at you for the person you choose to caress

It's not fair that I put my happiness in your hands

Hoping that I get a full day when you make your daily plans

It's not fair to her when you go home smelling like me

For her to think you had a rough day so you don't have to speak

It's not fair to her when we have late-night conversations while she sleeps

And in my heart all I want you to do chose me

It's not fair I sleep alone every night

That my body rejects any nigga that's not you on sight

It's not fair to me that I have to cherish the precious moments you grant me

Being last when I know I deserve,

I'm worth more than these crumbs you give me

What do you want from me…
Someone once said, "Whoever asked you to feel, you were chosen."
But the hand life has dealt me, I just wanted to fold it
Suppressing all the shit I've been through,
my story can change someone's perspective on life
The selfish, proud part of me never wanted the truth to come to light
Abused mentally and physically by ones who were supposed to love me
Raped by strangers who just wanted to hurt me
Raising a man who is my child who will never be capable of living alone
Broken and homeless, trying to call some place home
God said the storm is meant to make you strong
With all the rain and dark clouds I think 20 years is way too long
There for those who needed help
Took the shirt off my back, literally when I needed it, quiet as kept
Lost the only man who loved me unconditionally
Found myself in a string of men and women who only wanted sex from me
No real love or compassion or zest to be my one and only
I still go to sleep at night confused and lonely
Still I smile, I chat, I start over day after day
Is this it, Lord, me crying in my shower until I find another way
What do you want from me?
I'm a shell of what I used to be
Dismissed anyone's thoughts and opinions of how I should be
People take advantage of the kindness that they see
This is me…love me…or let me be

When I close my eyes…ummm, when I close my eyes
I feel your hands rubbing all over my thighs
The moisture from your lips whispering on the small of my back
Imagining your skin all oily and black
Massaging your fingers slowly on the bottom of my lips
Your beard brushing briefly on the tip of her lips
The warmth of your tongue caressing her pearl
Me slightly licking and biting your fingertips
Heels lunging through the top of the sunroof
You kissing her like you missed her and got something to prove
Turning you over on your back, catching your eyes
As I slowly creep between your thighs
Grazing your bulge lustfully across my face
Blowing out the candle on that invisible birthday cake
As our position switch I feel the passion of your thrust
There's no denying the chemistry between us
Feel me up with the sweet nectar of your vein
Finishing up with some pleasure-pleasing brain
I opened my eyes just to see
That the only one pleasing me is me
Was that real or was it make believe
That I'm in this entanglement and the only one getting hurt is me

Jay Z said it best: "What you eat don't make me shit"
And if you lose the will to fight that doesn't make me wanna quit
You and me live in two different realities
That's why I let you be you, now let me be me
Judge not lest ye be judged, says the word
So if I do something you don't agree with it's absurd
I want you to succeed, I want you to be great
What's easier in this world to do, love or hate
I'm all for empowerment if you want it or not
You can't get mad at the next person on how far they got
Maybe you don't have the will, maybe you don't see the way
Who am I to judge you, Rome wasn't built in a day
Oh, you too that, oh, you too this
Why should it matter to you, there's more than your way to exist
Moral of the story, keep your opinions to yourself
'Cause I'm pretty sure they would've asked if anyone needed your help

What do you think about when you close your eyes at night?
Is it ever about me…or is it always about your wife?
And when you touch her…do you ever think about me?
When you close your eyes…is it me that you see?
Did you feel those chills, when I pleasured myself today?
The way I feel about you…could you ever feel that way?
Do you know when you touch her…she instantly gets moist?
Do you see my body tremble at the sound of your voice?
Do you know she was invented just for you?
No one can fit my puzzle piece quite like you do
Secretly taken but extremely single
No one but you can make her cream and tingle
I'm going to enjoy every moment with you like it's my last
I hope you know you're the best I ever had

Tell me what those voices do, show me what those visions say
I wish I could crawl inside you just so you don't have to feel that way
No one understands you, they think your episodes are fake
But they don't see the confusion and that scared look upon your face
I know you don't want to be on this earth anymore
because you can't handle this pain
You tell me alcohol and drugs will numb the obstacles that are in your way
You're not my little boy no more and mentally you're not a capable young man
Who told you that nonsense, apparently this was God's plan
Explain what it's like to see and hear things that want to hurt you
Make enemies of your family and friends that just want to love you
I ask God every night why him, Lord, why my son
I guess this is not my battle but I believe this can be won
Give this to me, God, give my son a chance
Give him a life that he can understand
Do you know how it feels to think that any second
he can just give up and he'd be gone
I just want to trade places with him, I'd rather be withdrawn
He don't know you and sometimes he doesn't know me
It breaks a mother's heart to know that this is maybe who he will always be

She's the cake, I guess I'm the too
If I had one wish I would only choose you
It's you I wanna build with living in luxury
But it's her you go home to so your choice should be clear to me
I'm just a dirty little secret that no one should ever know
Stupid of me to fall for you but I can't just let you go
You described your ideal mate to me, that's sure not me on your list
I'm the complete opposite of what you want,
in your own words you don't want this
But every week I seem to see you for only an hour or two
Then you go home to the one who thinks you're faithful, kind, and true
Let me go if you don't want me, let me be someone else's trophy
Let the greatness that is me bless someone who is worthy
I no longer cry when you go home at night, I don't shed not one little tear
My actions spoke louder than my words, my love for you was sincere
Are you afraid to start over 'cause she was your ride or die
How do you look her in the eyes every day knowing you're living a lie
You can say you don't love me, you can say this is just our moment in time
She won, she can have you, it's no point trying to make you only mine

The only thing I require from a person is the ability to affect you day

If I'm not on your mind at least 50 percent of the time then I'll get out your way

If you don't wake up yearning for my touch then we will never be

Because I just want someone that does the same as me

If your day isn't complete until you hear my voice then why would you want me

If I can't make a bad day go away with just my love then I shouldn't be there anyway

If you don't wanna shoot my love in your veins so I truly be with you

If the thought of me doesn't get a rise out of you then just throw up the deuce

I don't want you to just love me, those are just words that seem to be forced

I want you to drink me up so I replenish your thirst

Your mind shouldn't even fathom the thought of not speaking with me, then we can't be

Stop wasting each of our time and just let it go

Because anything less than that is unacceptable, my worth I already know

Sitting here contemplating should I jump or not
Nowadays life is meaningless, once you're gone you're easily forgotten
I don't remember shit being this hard back then
When everyone did what they could to help you win
Knowing how it feels to be one check away from living on the street
Doing your best to survive, this shit is getting pretty bleak
I know struggle don't last always and it's hard not to be a statistic
But when you're down your whole life it's hard to keep being optimistic
Stay strong, hardship builds character
But what happens when you don't wanna wake up the morning after
I don't know how strong God wants me to be
'Cause when you look up lonely, depressed, and suicidal, in the dictionary
there's a picture of me
When you see me there's always a smile, kind words, positive motivation
But when I'm alone it's just self-deprivation
Usually there's a silver lining in the things I write
Not this one, I'm going into hiding, staying out of sight
I've broken down, there's nothing left for me to give, I'm tapped out
Just keep me in mind, when they ask you what mental illness is all about

I'm not equipped to being an afterthought
My presence is thunderous…fuck you, thought
My being lights up the fucking room
Although your existence in my life ended way too soon
If I treated you like an option then I could see
Putting me on the back burner, I would agree
But I treated you like a King, all Simba and shit
Fuck this relationship, fuck you, and ya bitch

I saw the potential in you the first moment I talked to you
Let me upgrade your way of thinking into the new you
She stifled your inner glow
You're in her shadow 'cause she didn't want you to grow
I want to elevate together like Bey and Hova
All you gotta say is yes and this nightmare is over
Let me entice your inner synergy
So there's no one in this world but you and me
Let me embrace that brilliant mind
My love for you is upfront, it's not that hard to find
I want us both to win, shit, we both the prize
I need you to feel appreciated and worthy of these earthly goods
Let's take this journey together, let's team up in these woods
Baby, when you succeed we succeed
And we can continue in ecstasy
What are you waiting, for shit to get better
Naw, she ain't that same bitch when you first met her
Her dream is where she at, what she already doing
I know you want more, what are you pursuing
I'm pursuing your love, so we can rip this world apart
I'm backing you, baby, 'cause you got my heart

Here I am back in this delusion of what appears to be love
Being second to a man that I put first
My heart is broken, it seems to be cursed
Why can't I find someone who is just for me
Instead of picking up this woman's old leftover wannabe
I want him to be mine from here until the end of time
But apparently it's not me who he wants
He makes it clear with every encounter
By me going home alone without him
I don't want to love him but my heart and my mind don't agree
Why is it not me, I wish it would be

I'm not that broad no more
You know, that broad that'll knock on the door
Tell your chick what I did to that nigga she looking for
Tell her you've been at my house in my bed between my legs
But I'm not that broad no more
If I was that broad, though,
I would take those condoms that we keep in the car
Take them to your bitch house, tell her we don't use those no more
If only I was that broad I would release all those videos, all those text messages, everything that you ever wrote me, and send it to your bitch
But I'm not that broad no more, oh my God if…if I were that broad I would take this match light up your house
Lucky for you I calmed the fuck down
Lucky for you I'm a fucking lady now
But if I was that broad, though…only if you knew

My beliefs have been compromised
My love for you have jeopardized
My entire existence
I saw the proof
I saw the beating of its little heart
I sat there and watched a piece of me die
It's easy for you to continue as if it never was
Live your life like we never were
My being was your adventure
I loved you and still do
The pain in my body isn't as hurtful as the pain in my heart
Knowing that we would never be
Let it go, live your life
Is what people tell me
But how when all I want is to be near you
Smell you, be within you
Never had I felt this way
Don't remember me without you
It's harmful, it's detrimental
I want you but it's one-sided
I guess I should let it die like our unborn

Your wife is lucky, she gets to go to sleep with you and wake up with you every day
She doesn't have to experience pain when you're away
I want for us to be like that
Knowing when you leave the house after work you'd come right back
I go to sleep and wake up with you on my mind, feeling broken inside
But when you ask how I'm doing I'm always fine
I fell in love with your intelligence before I fell in love with you
Knowing this is going to end horribly for me, I just don't know what to do
All I want is one full day and by night's end I'm in your arms
I tried to pull away but I get wrapped up in your charm
That smile, that body, oh my God, that sex
Makes it hard for any guy that wants to be next
I want to breathe you in and bask in our oneness
I want our bond to be blinding like gold that never tarnishes
When I close my eyes your face is all I see
And when I think of you my heart bleeds
I want to drink you in and get intoxicated
I want to lose my mind and forgot that I'm fornicating
You make my soul smile within
I sit and wonder about our life and when it would begin
I thought I would be fine being number two
But when you are in love with a married man what else are you supposed to do

Falling in love with what we do
Upset because I'm not who you're going home to
The way you touch my body, making me want more
Leaving me in pure ecstasy when you walk out my door
Side bitch, next bitch, call me what you like
If that bitch was doing her job you wouldn't be here tonight
Sometimes I don't want to close my eyes
Imagination so strong I still feel you between my thighs
Bodies thrusting, blood rushing through my veins
Moaning and trying to not to call the Lord's name in vain
Don't want this to end, keep playing with her like that
See if you can make her cry when you hit her from the back
Phone's ringing, is that yours or mine
Your girl can wait while you invade me from behind
Pulling my hair, choking me a bit
Trying not to gag on your enormous dick
Kissing me ever so gently, grabbing me by my waist
Lifting me high, sitting me on your face
Then off you go home to her, not me
Leaving me wanting more until the next time we meet

I want that forever type of love
That "I can't stop thinking about you" type of love
That "put your phone down" undivided kind of love
That almost impossible type of love

I want that "I can't be without you one day" type of love
That "I call you every day" type of love
That "it hurts when you're not with me" type of love
That unforgettable type of love

That "rub your shoulders" type of love
That "make you breakfast" kind of love
That "I want to wake up to every morning" type of love
That "it's hard to breathe without you" type of love

I want that "I got your password" type of love
That "leave everything on the table" type of love
That "leave a toothbrush at your place" type of love
That "watch you sleeping" type of love

I want that "morning text" type of love
That "lunch and dinner" kind of love
I want that "taking a shower together" type of love
That "I just want you near you" type of love

"I want to touch you all day" type of love
"I can't be away from you" type of love
That "meeting your friends and family" type of love
That one day "I Do" type of love

Nowadays you can't find that type of love
People aren't ready for that kind of love
Nothing but secrets and lies type of love
That "bullshit baby mama ex-girlfriend" type of love
That "let me hold something" type of love

Fuck that type of love

Unexpected memories from an unexpected world
Unexpected pregnancy from a scared young girl
Afraid and alone, raising two on her own
Finding strength in her children because their father is gone

Ignoring the rumors and gossip that is spread about her
Working as hard as she can to support her children and her
Overcame the obstacles that constantly got in her way
Although she's sad and alone she wants to see another day

Her children and her happiness, her reason to go on living
Unexpected births from experience are only hard in the beginning
So if there's one thing I could say to scared young girls
Be strong, don't give up because it's an unexpected world

Never giving up no matter what the consequences may be
Always working hard because I know what is best for me

Whatever it took I did with everything I have inside
I couldn't afford to fail so I didn't run and hide

I put my right foot forward and opened the door for opportunity
I know how hard it is to move ahead because nothing was handed to me

I had goals and made sure that I accomplished them all
I learned from my mistakes, that's the reason why we fall

When life gets hard and it feels like you're going to fall
Put your head up and get up off the wall

When it feels like everyone has turned their backs on you
Don't get discouraged, just do what you think you have to do

If you feel like you need to go right but all your friends are going left
Don't be a follower because no one can live your life but yourself

In life there are setbacks but they're there to make you strong
Remember, the Lord said that the rain doesn't last long

And if you still feel like you're at a standstill and your life is stuck
Just do what Tupac said and KEEP YOUR HEAD UP

When I look in the mirror let me tell you what I see
A beautiful, intelligent young woman posing to be me
A strong individual that wants to be set free
A scared little girl hid deep inside of me

My reflection reveals more than the eyes can see
It reveals hurt, pain, hurt, and images that used to be me
Maybelline cannot cover hidden scars that don't appear
Scars which were inflicted by pain, hurt, and fear

The mirror is like an ocean, you can see beauty far away
It's also like sunset, everlasting beauty here to stay
So tell me what you see in the mirror, what does your reflection reveal?
Remember to keep a positive thought and make sure what you feel is real

I once thought that family were supposed to be like what I saw on TV
All loving and warmhearted, I guess the only one who thought that was me
The second of my mother's children, the fifth of my dad's
Being confused and left out, I was the only person I had

Not knowing how to fit in with my siblings and felt like the black sheep
Only visions of a normal childhood I had in my sleep
One side of my family are peaceful and calm
The other, only fuss and fight, it's like the war in Vietnam

It gets harder day by day, not knowing who to turn to
I can't ask for help, because I'm afraid they wouldn't know what to do
So to myself again I turn to and put my thoughts down on this sheet
Hoping and praying that there's a middle ground where everyone can sit and meet

I'm pretty sure my family isn't the only one that's screwed up this way
I just hope that the way I feel about this will fade one day
So until then this is how I feel
I hope they take my feelings into consideration, because this pain is so real

Cosmic signs of this galaxy
Enhanced my visions of reality
Things that were destined for me
Is how Mother Nature wanted it to be

Future as bright as the North Star
Kinetic energy leading me to where you are
With wide arms and an open heart
Knowledge of knowing God is telling me how to start

This journey of finding peace with myself
And reassurance that he will be there if I need help
That what lies before me is a gift from God
He knows the decision that I had to make and he knows that it was hard

Ten little fingers and ten little toes
She has my grandmother's features and she has my little nose
Big, beautiful brown eyes and a beautiful soul
No one can predict the future, only God knows

This unexplainable feeling that I have inside
The questionable tears as I cried
How could something so loving and fragile come out of me?
Then I heard a voice saying this is your gift from me
When I think of you tonight
I'll remember how things were so perfect and right
And how things were meant to be
The strong bond between you and me

Every night is harder than the night before
Hoping and wishing you would walk through the door
Kissing and embracing me like you used to do
Because at this very moment I'm only thinking of you

Nothing is better than hearing your voice and seeing your face
The love we have is strong and can never be erased
Because at this very moment my heart belongs to you
You're like my best friends and I'll always remain true

So when I close my eyes tonight and my thoughts are all on you
I'll remember everything you said to me and everything we do
Because at this very moment I'm lonely, it's true
But I will always remember how much you cared and that's why I love you

I close my eyes and remember the sweet smell of your breath
Lying in my bed, touching the pillow and your presence I still felt
Putting your picture beside me so it feels like you're right here
Remembering when you told me with you in my life,
I should have no reason to fear
Now I'm here alone with only memories of the way it used to be
Tears falling from my eyes, making it impossible to see
I guess it's true when they say never missing someone until they're gone
And realizing without you in my life the journey for completion has just begun

It used to be us against the world and now it's just me
I feel like an endangered forest with only one tree
There's no one to laugh at the ridiculous riddles that I may say
I don't think you know how much this is killing me
not to see your face each day
But this is how you wanted it to be
You didn't think we were ready or was it you? Just weren't ready for me
However it may be you're no longer here,
you left me to figure things out by myself
I wonder if you're hoping that I get confused, and ask for help

I get sidetracked when I think of us when we were two
Surprising me every day, there were no limits to the things you would do
Maybe that's why it's so hard for me to let go
Secretly I felt like you were the only one that was meant for me,
the only thing I knew
Getting over you may take a little time
I will always love you and in my heart you're still mine
Time heals all wounds, especially the wound you left in my heart
I understand this is what you felt you had to do
so I don't blame you on your part

Can we sit down and discuss the way you treat me
Last week you bruised my shoulder and blacked my eye and I could barely see
Yesterday I wore so much make-up I looked like a runway clown
And you always call me out my name and putting me down
I know you love me because you tell me this every day
But I don't think love is supposed to hurt, I think you can treat me another way
See, I'm tired of lying to people about how I got hurt or how I got a black eye
I'm afraid that you might kill me one day, do you really want me to die?
Last month you broke my leg in three different places and broke my nose too
Then you want to propose to me, do you really think I should marry you?
You act like things are going to change if I say I Do
I don't think you truly understand what you put me through
I'm tired of crying myself to sleep at night
I'm tired of waking up to a drunken man who always want to fight
Last night you said you hit me because I didn't take out the trash
This morning I woke up and all the windows on my car were bashed
My mother came by at the beginning of the week
I didn't have my make-up on and she almost freaked
She said she didn't raise me to be disrespected by any man
But I tried to comfort her by saying I'm doing the best that I can
I'm tired of giving you chance after chance
I'm starting to think you don't know how to be a real man
Don't look out the window because those cops are here to pick up you
And in case you didn't get the memo, this means we're through

I'm writing this to you while you're in lockdown
Everyone is talking about our jailhouse romance all around town
They ask me who I'm with and I say that I'm in love with you
But I see what they say, our freaky phone calls just won't do
I remember when my phone bills were less than a hundred dollars
I'm just going to have to drop you a line…dude, I'll holla
See, what can you offer me while you're behind bars
Your best friend came over the other day in his brand-new car
He said he can give me what I miss
But his touch don't feel like yours and I don't think I'm ready for this
Your letters are getting steamy and every page is a little wet
I hope that's perspiration from writing, I hope the heat is making you sweat
I can't keep spending money trying to see you each week
I can't take the way you look at me every time I speak
I can't help but wonder when you get out your love will go astray
And beating myself up, asking why did you do me this way
So behind bars is the only way our love will remain true
So this will be the last letter, 'cause I don't want to be with you

Remember back then, when men used to hold the doors
Court you and made you feel special instead of acting like it's a chore
Remember serenades under your window at night
Under the oak tree beautiful singing in the moonlight
Getting to know each other before you bed
Having children after you wed
Remember when men used to say sweet nothings in your ear
Having butterflies in your stomach every time he's near
What happened to those days, I mean the way we were then
We let men disrespect us, that's when self-hatred begins
Let them think that what they say goes
And every move we made they had to be the first to know
You start putting yourself down, saying that you're fat
Oh, do you ever wish you can have those days back
Instead of trying your best to please him
It's time to turn the table, it's the new millennium
Women are in control so let your spirit run free
Tell them that you don't care what they think of me
As long as you love yourself and make the best of who you are
Because the way we are isn't too far
If he wants you he can wait
Tell him what you expect him to put on the plate
Because it's all about you, what you say goes
Say it loud and clear, let that man know
Pondering over a memory that didn't last forever
Reminiscing of all the stormy nights that we had spent together
My heart's so empty as tears begin to pour
Just hoping, just wishing that one day you will walk through that door
For me to find the right one feels like eternity
Remembering the way we used to laugh while you were holding me
Regretting the day you left, the day you walked out my life
The way I felt, wanting to die, that was the day you kissed me goodbye
It's too late now, you can't relive the past
But our love was strong and it was meant to last
So for you, my love, it's not forever goodbye
Our paths will cross again and we will be together till the day we die

I don't have to flaunt my sexuality
I'm a private person, I don't like to bring attention to me
I love that I can be myself
I don't need any unwanted outside help

If I was ashamed of being me
Then I have a bigger issue to see
But not shouting it out to the world
Just seems right for this private girl

So don't assume that you can figure me out
If you want to know ask me what I'm all about
Because no one knows better than me
What this private girl wants to see

I don't change like the weather every day
I didn't say if I was straight or if I'm gay
Because I'm a private girl, can't you see
I just love and enjoy being me

Didn't you know I see you every day?
Were you brought up that way?
You never seem to wash your hair
Is that lice I see crawling under there?
I saw you scratch a couple of times
I'm not trying to be mean, just telling you what's on my mind
Because B.O. is everywhere
Didn't you notice me move over here because you were over there?
I believe teeth are supposed to be white
Usually you can see them at night
Why do your teeth look like the sun?
I just started, sweetheart, I'm not even done
It's the middle of the week, shouldn't you shower?
Because funk grows stronger by the hour
If you took a bath you wouldn't have that itch
Hopefully, baby girl, you wouldn't have that sour stench
I know you don't like coming outside like that
I'm surprised your mom didn't snatch that ass back
Especially when you scratch yourself on the street
Remember not to touch people that you meet
Some places have public showers for people like you
Just don't pass washing that ass, whatever you do
This is the nicest way that I can say
Your personal hygiene should be taken care of every day
One day you might meet someone who isn't as nice as me
I'm trying to be as blunt as I can possibly be
Because I feel it's my duty to tell you that you smell
It's under your nose so you should know that stench well
So take what I'm saying in a positive way
You shouldn't smell like that each day
They say the first one to smell you is you
So when you wake up make sure the shower is the first thing you do
Because it's not natural to smell like that
So remember every day to wash that musty-ass cat

Men, I would really like to know how it feels
Raping a woman, hearing her scream, having her squeal
Do you ever think about putting your feet in her shoes?
Having someone invading your body, doing what you do
How do you feel seeing tears running down her face?
Having her heart beating and pounding like she just ran a race
You ever think about her family or if she has kids?
You understand you're hurting more than that person when you do what you did
What about those bruises and scars that will be with her for life
How do you justify yourself, that what you're doing is right
What about those disease-conscious people
Ever think about getting AIDS or other STDs that are lethal
You can say look at what she's wearing or how she's walking
You ever listen to what you say and how you're talking
Do you feel guilty? Do you want to repent for your sins?
People like you don't deserve to be walking,
you should be locked up like chickens in pens
When you read this poem and you feel like crying get a tissue
Because this is bigger than all of us, this is to let you know that rape is an issue

The Lord has granted my wish, it came true
The very first moment I laid eyes on you
And every night I prayed for a good man
To take care of me the very best he can

To love and cherish plus honor me too
After the vows to say "I Do"
In front of God our family and friends
We pledge our love till the end

In sickness and health I will love you
And in my heart will always be true
So to my love, the love of my life
I would be more than honored to be your beautiful wife

If only I had someone who loved me and cared
And every time I needed him he would always be there
To honor and cherish me until the day I die
Who loved my children and never told a lie

If only there was someone out there who feels the way I do
To only be loved by someone and have that love be true
To sit and share our feelings and what we want in life
To have him get on one knee and ask me to be his wife

If only that special someone was looking for me too
If only he would ask I would certainly say I do
I want a love that I can cherish forever
I want us to be happy and grow old together

If only I didn't have to dream of the perfect man
Instead of having him here holding me hand
I guess in life I was meant to be alone
So my search for a loving mate will have to go on

If only in life it didn't have to be this way
To love someone, to lose someone, there ends a dreadful day
Living a lonely, loveless life is what I fear
Only wanting someone to love and have him be here

If only I had the power to create the perfect man
I guess a lot of women would want that...I could understand
But I'm tired of being lonely, I'm tired of feeling blue
Only to want that special someone to say I love you

Do you remember when we used to play?
Laughing and running till that one dreadful day
That day when everything changed
When our sunshine turned into rain

Do you remember that day in the car way back then?
When some drunk man hit us and my life had to end
Even though I was gone my spirit was still there
And I'm going to continue watching you because I care

Do you remember me, Katrina was my name
I destroyed lives and a beautiful city that will never be the same
I came like a thief in the night
I brought nothing but darkness, now I leave you to find the light

Do you remember me? I'm the AIDS epidemic, the one with no cure
I take lives of the bad, good, the evil, and the pure
I have no conscience, I have no shame
I put fear in your heart and make you take the blame

Do you remember me? I was once inside you
I guess I had you scared and confused because you didn't know what to do
So you went to this place and when you came out, there was no me
Why didn't you give me to someone else, there was a lot I wanted to see

Remember me? The coronavirus that is deadly as can be
Taken out hundreds of thousands of people like you and me
Shut down the world, had you scared to leave your homes
Wearing masks, creating vaccines to this virus that was unknown

If you remember me, remember me well
Never forget what it took for you to get up after you fell
Don't let your dreams and your life be put on hold
Because the world as we learned to love is getting cold

I brought up a lot of topics near to heart
It was kind of hard for me because I didn't know how to start
But they were on my mind and there's no other way to express how I feel
I was trying to be honest and tried to keep it real

Nowhere to run, nowhere to hide
I'm poverty stricken, I just want to die
Society overlooks me and nobody cares
I call on the Lord because he's the only one there
I call on my mother, my father too
They say they can't help me, there's nothing they can do
So the alley is my bedroom, the ground is my bed
I put a stack of old papers as a pillow for my head
A cardboard box as my shelter, thrown-out scraps for my food
I take a shower when it rains and wash my clothes too
I have friends on the street, they're my family now
I don't know why I'm here, I keep asking myself how
People pass me on the street and look at me in shame
They say I'm just a bum and I have no one but myself to blame
But no one could have predicted the outcome of my life
I had beautiful children and a lovely wife
But they all left me when things went bad
I lost everything I worked for, everything I had
There's no looking back now, everything's gone
Why didn't people tell me this would happen when things go wrong
So I'm finished with this story, this sad little song
The streets are my home now, apparently where I belong
If only had I listened to the people who cared
Now I only talk to the Lord, he's the only one that's there

Oh, you don't like what you see in me
So why don't you buy what you want me to wear then
My clothes represent me
Free-spirited, self-loving, not worried about what anyone say or think about me
If I can fit it, then I'm going to wear it
If I can afford it, then I'm going to buy it
If you don't like it, look the other way
Because how I look in the mirror, baby, I just made my own day
I don't need you to say, that would look tight if I was a little thinner
I'm not a rookie in this game, you act like I'm a beginner
If I can pull it off, then you should be glad
Big girl showing off, I can see why you're mad
My self-image is not what you think of me, but how I think of myself
If you took your thoughts off me, then you'll see you're the one who needs help
If it makes you feel good by trying to put me down
I have something else on my agenda and don't have the time or energy to frown

I just need to release some thoughts that are on my mind
It might take a while, I have to search deep so I can find
Something worthy enough to write
That's why I stepped outside tonight
I'm swimming in a pool of disappointment and grief
Looking over my life and feeling this overwhelming disbelief
Remembering when there was a time when life was too hard to bear
Gazing in the sky, asking the Lord if there was one less life he could spare
I always thought that I was too young to have went through the things I have
Just thinking this was the hand I was dealt, the wrong road to my path
I just thought things were different now, I thought I strayed away from my past
Only to realize that I was dreaming because good things never last
To think that I put everything behind me laid everything to rest
Thought I talked about everything and got it all off my chest
I guess deep down everyone wishes life was a fairytale,
that good things do come true
Kinda like the way I looked or thought about you
I guess I was destined to live the way I do in a world like this
To find my prince to wake me up from a deep, dark sleep with a long, nice kiss
But life is full of disappointments and I learned that hard
So there's only one thing to do and that's pray to God
So it's time to open my eyes and see people
for what they really are and stop making excuses
To start thinking positive things about my life and that it's not useless

I don't recall you having that before
I didn't see that in your hands as you walked through my door
Do I have to put my name on everything that's mine?
Because my brown bag has never been that hard to find

Do you want me to pat you down before you leave?
Just don't plunder with my stuff, please
I don't go to your place and take what's yours
So get that idea out of your mind when you walk through my doors

If you can't keep to yourself don't come around me
Because the cops, sweetheart, you will see
So if you have something that is rightfully mine
I'd advise you to put it back before I kick your behind

It's kind of hard to write from your heart when your mind is filled with clutter
Sometimes I want to go inside and cry, close all my blinds and shutters

Hurting from inside of me begins to peak and wants to be set free
So much pain and discomfort, I can't believe that this came out of me

Trying to hide from the world and show them a not-so-true sight
Trying to cover up my pain, keep them hidden so that they can't see the light

I try to calm down and start thinking of some good deed that I've done
Sitting in the corner looking in the mirror,
feeling worse 'cause I know they think they've won

But good things come to those that wait, good things indeed
So I have to sit down and focus on what I want, my hopes and my needs

This is just something that I wrote to clear my head so that my mind can breathe
So that I can sit down and feel better,
not feeling so much pain as I continue to read

Life can be hard, but I taught myself to survive, you have to be strong
So I let my mind do all the work as my hand just played along

I know one day I'll have my turn to rise above the rest
Until I do, I'll sit down and become stronger,
so when that day comes I can do and be at my best
Last night I stayed up and cried
I cried for everyone who is living and everyone who died
I cried for all the homeless people who have to live on the street
I cried for everyone I bumped into and everyone I meet
I cried for my children and I cried for me
I cried for all the deaf people and the ones who cannot see
I cried for people who are behind bars
I cried for those who want nothing more than to be a star
I cried for people who are very depressed
I cried for those who are under stress
I cried for the people who died September the eleventh
I cried for their souls to go to heaven
I cried for premature babies, their moms and dads
I cried for those people who thought their marriages would last
I cried for soldiers that are overseas
And when I finished I wondered…did anyone cry for me?

Cupid should have known better than to aim that arrow at you
How can a person possibly split their heart in two?
Someone always gets hurt in the end
Cupid should have known that shit, before it begin
A heart that's already spoken for never lasts
Cupid should have known that from the past
Wasted tears, thoughts, and emotions on a heart that someone already claimed
It's not Cupid's fault, I have to take all the blame
Looking for something, in someone, who had what I was looking for
Never can settle, always looking for more
So when Cupid's dust finally fades away
I guess until I can say goodbye, maybe we will meet another day
So farewell, now my heart can breathe
Soft-spoken words, which put my heart at ease

Look, I'm getting off this roller-coaster of emotion that you have me on
I just got rid of someone that had me singing this sad song
Get your shit together before you try to be with me
Because us being one is just not meant to be
You're going through things, well, shit, so am I
Damn, I pick the wrong week to stop smoking, I need something to get me by
I can't shut off my feelings like flipping a switch
A week has went by and I haven't heard from you since
You told me not to give up on you and you just need a little time
Find another one to spit game to, tell that hoe some tired lines
'Cause just like this so-called relationship, I'm cutting you out
All that lying and playing games is not what I'm about
So kick rocks…I'm calling it a day
I used to feel something for you, now I just don't feel the same way

Stab me in the back as soon as you can
Then be all in my face like we're best friends
Call me crying because you're having problems with you man
I hope he beats your ass, 'cause phony bitches I can't stand
When I needed you, you couldn't help me
Now I know why, now I see
I knew he was fucking around, I just didn't have proof
Now I know that bitch he was fucking…was you
Enemies, who need enemies, with friends like you
All the dirt you did, I held your secrets true
One false move, stupid bitch, and you're through
So, how many other women niggas fucking you
Fight, no bitch, I'm too cute to fight
But keep trying me, little bitch, I just might

I see myself in the mirror, I used to look a different way
I used to be a loving mom, with my children I did play
I used to be a respectable member of my community
But it's sad that this is what drugs did to me
I lost my children, because I lost my soul
I'm addicted to drugs is what I've been told
Nothing on my mind, but the thought of getting high
I'm not concerned of an overdose or the fact that I could die
I'm so blinded to the way I've become to be
Now my body doesn't even belong to me
I sell myself so I can get a quick fix
I see so many people ending up in a ditch
But this crack is too strong for me to beat
I search for my dealers along the street
I shoot up, I snort, anything to get high
I even ask for money from people passing by
I found out I have H.I.V.
And trying to think who could have given it to me
The list is too long, I'm sad to say
But the addiction's so strong, I don't care either way
I still trick for my high, infecting the world
Too sick to get help, I used to not be this girl
I find myself behind steel bars
For going up to an undercover in his car
Maybe this time will help me see
The ugly person I became to be
If this is the only way I can get help
Because I know I can't do it by myself
But what will happen when I'm free?

Will my addiction take over me?
Will I sleep around too high?
How will I go about getting by?
Will I ever think about the consequences of my way?
Will I ever see my children all grown up one day?
I don't want to be this person that I now see
Because once upon a time this used to not be me
As I glanced around the room I saw a person from the street
She began to walk toward me
She started telling me her life and how it used to be
And what her addiction caused her not to see
She noticed she hit rock bottom when she got high around her kids
Not realizing that they knew exactly what she did
Seeing their faces blurred in her sight
Not feeling the same as she kissed them goodnight
But she got help, got help in the nick of time
Only God knows what was on her mind
She's doing better, almost a year clean
Trying to help those by telling them
what she's been through and what she's seen
She got herself together and her kids are happy too
Because they saw what drugs made their mother do
Her life she shares as a glimpse of her past
She said drugs made her days fade fast
So to those who need help and don't know how to get it
If you're tired of the way your life is and you just want to quit
Look up to the Lord and ask for help to get through
Because if it can happen for her, it can happen for you

Hope for the best and expect the worst, they say
Believe me, that's what I was doing today
My heart was pounding so hard like I had ran a race
You could see the sweat beads running down my face

Looking for one answer that could only make my day
One word could only make me turn away
I feel the tears waiting to come down
It's so quiet, I heard every little sound

Will it be yes or will it be no
Will I be walking out the door?
Waiting for the answer, what will it be?
Will it be the best thing for me?

People watching, I feel their eyes
One poor woman began to cry
I heard an answer but it wasn't yes
How the hell did I get in this mess?

I really think I should've waited
No matter how long we had been dating
Too young to really know what I was getting into
Never can get my innocence back no matter what I do

He said close my eyes and he would be gentle and go slow
Not wanting to be there, I just didn't let him know
It seemed like I waited an eternity for my first time
But after what happened, I must have been out of my mind

It wasn't all what I had dreamt it would be
Maybe if I would've waited it could've been differently
I really think underage sex is kind of overrated
The way he kept touching my body made me feel degraded

He really wasn't the right one for me
But it took that experience to open my eyes so I could see
That was a decision that I should've taken seriously
But I made that choice to do it, which was all on me

The feeling of being totally alone
Even when there's people around or you're on the phone
It's the feeling that's deep inside of you
And it feels like nothing can soothe it; nothing you can do
It's that overwhelming feeling of emptiness
While you're examining your life, asking why it had to be like this
It's like the world's one big struggle and it seems
like it's always tearing you down
Even when you try to bear life in a positive way it always seems to turn around
In a negative downbeat sort of way with an attitude, like why?
Why? Should I see another day?
In a world that's filled with hardship and grief
While trying to understand your life with people around in awe and disbelief
It's that vanquished feeling of trying to do things in a certain more positive way
With people on the street selling crack to our kids as they do this day by day
It's that dark empty space in your mind where you can hide from the ig-
norance of this world
It's like an oyster holding tight to its one and only pearl
It's that summer getaway spot in your mind where you can only go
It's that make-believe place where you are the boss
with people you don't even know
It's that safe, comfortable spot where you are the only individual and no
one treads to go
It's that make-believe place where there's a large sign that reads DO NOT
ENTER so everyone else knows
That this is the place you hide yourself
from the world so that you can be totally alone
So let everyone you know you won't be answering any two-ways,
any texts, or any phones
It's that dark, quiet corner you go to, to read a book or talk to the Lord
To let him know that the life he had granted you is always on board
It's that area you can go when you get stressed out over materialistic things
that are thrown your way
It's that place where you go where you don't care what people do or what
they might say
It's just that way…ALONE

Back then there were only visions of what could be
Everyone thought they knew what was best for me
Always telling me to go here or go there
Not knowing who I could trust, I wasn't fully aware

It felt like life was standing on hold
I was like a child waiting for a story to be told
Because I wasn't living my life for me
I was trying to live up to what they wanted me to be

Now that I'm older and trying to do things my way
I found out it's harder and I can't wait for the end of the day
I now know that they were trying to shield me from the pain of rejection
Having pushed everyone away, now I feel so neglected

It takes knowledge and patience to get ahead in this world today
Now I'm left wondering if I would ever have it my way
Bleak as it may be, I still have hope for my life
My future is left up to me and I feel like I paid a hefty price

Pushed everyone away who loved me and who I loved too
To get where I wanted to go, I felt like that's what I had to do
I just hope my future reflects what I've been through in the past
And I hope I finally get what I want at last

Do you know how it feels to want something
so badly it hurts to even to think about it?
I understand now how slaves wanted freedom enough to die behind it
I sit behind this door and I know there's no way out
Not having control over anything I do, let me tell you all about

How I was stripped of all my pride and depression stepped in
No matter how I look at it, I should have changed my life back then
I wouldn't be sitting behind this door waiting for a helping hand
Tired of blaming all my problems on that same white man

Who had everything to do with the problems of today
Lock you up without asking is there anything more you would like to say
Sitting alone I think of things that could have been
If only I knew what I know now back then

Too young to go through this, too old to act like a child
I just know I've been depressed so long, I've forgotten how to smile
Longing for a chance to see the brightness of the day
All I can do is remember how it was and ask for forgiveness while I pray

Life for me is not as simple
A disturbed individual seeking approval
A lifeless child crying out loud
Without a soul to hear it

Life isn't at all peaches and cream
The world is filled with people who are devious and mean
With those who want to control you
And with people who aren't too willing to teach

If you think about it…that four-letter word
In your brain what does it mean?
So therefore what is life?

I opened my eyes
And saw nothing
I opened my ears
And heard nothing
I opened my mouth
And said nothing
The sun burnt my eyes
So I could not see
The thunder pierced my ears
So I could not hear
The pain broke my heart
So I could not feel
The fear got my soul
So I could not talk
A person of peace
Helped the inner me
A person of passion
Helped the outer me
I reached down deep
To find myself

Now I like me

Many people have demons that they need to overcome
Try to ask God for help so they could walk in his kingdom
Because some problems are so huge that they take over you
Until you are ready to change there's nothing any person can do

But pray that you help yourself from within
Because no one on earth is without sin
I can't even try to imagine how it could be
To have something so strong take over me

And I pray to God each and every day
That I continue to never go astray
And to those I feel bad for you
Because some don't know what the Lord can do

He gave us his son so that we could all be free
For him to die on the cross for you and me
So if there's any questions about real unconditional love
Just ask the Lord, he'll show you what he's made of

Pondering over a memory that didn't last forever
Reminiscing of all the stormy nights that we had spent together

My heart's so empty as tears began to pour
Just hoping, just wishing that one day you will walk through that door

For me to find the right one feels like eternity
Remembering the way we used to laugh while you were holding me

Regretting the day you left, the day you walked out of my life
The way I felt wanting to die, that was the day you kissed me goodbye

It's too late now, you can't relive the past
But our love was strong and it was meant to last

So for you, my love, it's not forever goodbye
Our paths will cross again and we will be together till the day we die

I think I told you this once or twice
I'm involved with someone and leaving him for you wouldn't be nice
I do admit having mixed feelings for you
But acting on those feelings is something I can't do

You make me want to sing like Erykah Badu
In that song, "now what am I supposed to do"
I think about you every day on the spot
Embracing my lover, thinking of you I should not

So I'm telling you this before it goes too far
Our love for each other is like an untouchable star
But I know that God brought this man from above
So what we have here has to be forbidden love

No one can make my mind change from bad to good by a brush of the hand
Who can put a smile on my face when I'm down…only my man

Your smile warms my heart
I get that feeling of togetherness that no one can part

My blood rushes through my body by just the tone of your voice
The only thing I can do is love you without a choice

It's amazing how your touch soothes my mind
I believe you broke the mold because you truly are one of a kind

I thank God for putting you in my life and blessing me with your grace
I feel nothing but love and joy just by looking upon your face

That's all I can say about the way I feel
I want you to know that I love you…and that, my friend, is real

Follow the rose petals as I walk in the door
White ones and red ones spread out on the floor
A glass a wine, a note that reads
Drink this, get undressed, and meet me on the bed
Into the bedroom, I did as the note said
A present on the bed, another note that read
Slip into this blindfold too
Because I want you to feel, not see what I'm about to do
Turning me over as you massage my back
Rubbing my shoulders…ooh, I like that
Feeling your tongue all over me
Wanting to take the blindfold off so that I can see
To feel your hands on my thighs
Touching me gently, kissing my eyes
Laying my body down with grace
Slowly kissing my face
As your clothing hits the floor one article at a time
Only can guess what you're thinking, what's on your mind
Long kisses from foot to head
Not skipping any place while we settle in our bed
For all the freaky things for us to do
You accomplished them all, didn't you
As I feel the you thrush inside of me
Touching your body as you embrace my inner mystery
Thinking of only my pleasure
You go down searching for my hidden treasure
Reaching the spot that gets me wet
Full of ecstasy as we both are through
We start over, doing what we do

This is the end, farewell I have to say
If this book sells well, I'll see you another day

I hope my thoughts brought hope and joy into your lives
Just remember, when things get rough just look up in the sky

Because what I've learned all my years here
That life is worth living and sometimes it's alright to shed some tears

Made in the USA
San Bernardino, CA
26 February 2013

Retire Rich

— and —

How to Work for Uncle Sam

Randall P. Hallier, CFP®

CFP® and CERTIFIED FINANCIAL PLANNER™ are certification marks owned by the Certified Financial Planner Board of Standards, Inc. These marks are awarded to individuals who successfully complete the CFP Board's initial and ongoing certification requirements.

Randall P. Hallier is a registered representative and offers advisory services and securities through LPL Financial, member FINRA/SIPC.

Contents

In the preparation of this book, every effort has been made to offer the most current and correct information possible. Nonetheless, inadvertent errors can occur and tax, benefits, and legislation often change.

Further, the information contained in this text is intended to afford general guidance to Federal Employees as well as their spouses and beneficiaries. Accordingly, the information in this book is not intended to serve as financial planning, legal, accounting, or tax advice. If financial, legal, investment, tax or retirement planning advice is required, readers are encouraged to consult with professional advisors.

Acknowledgements

This book is the product of many people, many more than I will have the opportunity to name. I want to thank the Federal Employees and their families who have extended the extraordinary privilege to me to act as their personal financial planner and trusted advisor. I also wish to thank the entire staff and clients of Retirement Plus, Inc. Without their help and patience, this book would not have been possible. Special thanks to Jessica Culpepper, MBA, and Sandy Samuelsen for their tireless efforts.

I would also like to thank Marie Swift, my relentless marketing coach and publicist, who never lost faith in me and this project, as well as my adopted mentors Randy Gardner, Nick Murray, and Bill Swift.

My thanks are also extended to my family including parents, siblings and grandparents whose work ethic taught me all I needed to know about the benefits of hard work and paying attention.

Finally, to Nancy Housh, my lovely fiancé and volunteer project manager: Thank you for your love, dedication, and patience.

~ Randy Hallier, CFP®

Foreword
by Randy Gardner

This book contains timely advice from Randall P. Hallier, CFP®, among the nation's top advisors on government retirement and employee benefits programs. For more than twenty years, Randy has delivered educational workshops and personal financial advice to thousands of people. He is widely known for his work with federal employees and government agencies.

Randy Hallier has continually impressed me over the years. Whether he is planning a client's future in the office, delivering a financial workshop at an employer-sponsored location, or teaching the masses through his radio show appearances, he is the consummate professional, always putting his clients' interests first. He is the embodiment of the term "client-centric" advisor — that I think all clients should demand when seeking or working with a financial advisor.

In my own work as a financial educator, I advise people to select financial planners based on The Five Cs: competent, current, comfort, caring, and cost. I have never met an advisor who is more conscientious than Randy about delivering on The Five Cs. He ensures his recommendations are appropriate for the client, suited to the times, and based on current best practices. Randy's wit and affable manner immediately puts clients at ease in a way that earns their trust and confidence. With regard to cost, Randy's pioneering efforts in the delivery of all the segments of financial planning — life insurance and risk mitigation, investment selection and management, tax, retirement, and estate planning in a one-stop format — are a testament to his concern for his clients' pocketbooks and busy schedules. This book reflects Randy's focus on The

Five Cs — it offers timely, relevant, and client-centered advice in a direct, personal manner similar to his approach in his educational workshops and private client engagements.

While many planners will rattle off the names of their celebrity clients, Randy prides himself on working extensively with federal employees. He is quick to point out that:

- The federal government is the largest employer in the world.

- Federal employees are highly educated, hard working, dedicated and proud of the role they play in the delivery of services to the American people.

- The benefit system, while complex, is comprehensive and uniquely tailored to the government's mission and the employees' needs.

His familiarity with government programs, obtained from years of study, delivery of workshops, and experience working with federal employees, oozes from every idea-filled page.

As this book goes to press, the world is in the throes of the most severe recession encountered since the Great Depression. Major companies have failed. The markets in 2008 declined by 40%. Housing prices have declined in the midst of record foreclosures. Unemployment is hovering around 10%. Government spending and deficits are at all time highs. Individuals are shaken as they hesitate to save, invest, retire, own a home, and make any other major financial decision. Randy's book addresses those concerns for federal employees by guiding them through the major financial planning questions with timeless answers.

In short, this book should be on every federal employee's bookshelf. It weaves solid financial planning advice with explanations of how federal employees can take advantage of the extensive benefit system available to them to accomplish what we all want — a worry-free, financially independent future.

~ Randy Gardner, JD, LLM, MBA, CPA, CFP®

Tax and Estate Planning Columnist for *The Journal of Financial Planning* and coauthor of *101 Tax Saving Ideas* and *The Tools and Techniques of Income Tax Planning*

About the Author

Randall P. Hallier, CFP®, is recognized as one of the leading experts in the field of financial and retirement planning for government employees. He has led hundreds of training sessions nationwide on a variety of topics related to retiring from government employment.

Randy has worked with nearly every department of the federal government including the Federal Bureau of Investigation; the Bureau of Alcohol, Tobacco, and Firearms; the Department of Agriculture; the Environmental Protection Agency; the United States Postal Service; and many others. As president and founder of Kansas-based Retirement Plus, Inc., an SEC Registered Investment Advisory firm, and its sister company, Financial Workshops, LLC, he has been providing financial planning and investment advice to public sector employees for more than 25 years.

This is not your parents' government pension plan.

Introduction

Myth Busting!

Are you a government worker? If so, this book was written specifically for you! Over the years, I have worked with numerous government workers—policemen, firefighters, aviation safety inspectors, museum specialists, economists, administrators, and other local, state, and federal government employees. It has been my goal to help them—and now you—overcome a pernicious and persistent myth about government employment. This myth is perpetuated by workers in the public sector and believed by many who work in the private sector. What is it? It is the belief that:

> *Federal employees' pension benefits are so generous that people who work for the government don't have to worry about saving for retirement.*

The unfortunate consequence of this myth is that many government employees think their pension plans will provide enough income for them to live comfortably after they retire—and that may not be the case. The consequences for people who buy into this myth are serious. If you're one of them, you may discover—in your 50s or early 60s—that you have inadequately prepared for retirement and are at risk of outliving your retirement savings. This may mean you have to work for more years than you'd expected, change your lifestyle after retirement, or make some sacrifices so you can save enough to reach your retirement goals.

On the other hand—if you don't accept the myth as reality—then you have an unparalleled opportunity. You have a chance to work for Uncle Sam and retire rich! And that's what this book is all about. The federal government has a generous retirement program, but you can only reap the rewards of the program if you understand the benefits available to you, make informed choices, and meet the requirements.

Get your facts straight

Did you know there are two pension programs offered by the federal government? There are. If you have been in government service for a long time, you might participate in the Civil Service Retirement System (CSRS). If you joined the government after 1983, it's likely that you participate in the Federal Employees Retirement System (FERS). If you don't know which program you participate in, then you need to find out—pronto!

Did you know each of these programs has six different retirement possibilities? Before you can choose the one best suited to your needs, you need to understand the options available to you.

Did you know there is a special savings program available to government employees? It allows you to set aside additional savings for retirement, thereby benefitting from tax deferral. The government will also make contributions to the accounts of many employees who save through the program.

Did you know you can retire with health insurance, life insurance, and long-term care insurance? You can, as long as you meet certain eligibility requirements.

Did you know some government employees qualify to receive Social Security and Medicare benefits? Do you qualify to receive them? It's important to know before you retire.

Do you know how the Government Pension Offset works? Are you familiar with the Windfall Elimination Provision and Social Security earnings limitation rules?

If you are not familiar with some or all of these things, don't worry. This book will provide you with information you need to plan your retirement and leave government service with the highest income and most valuable benefits package available to you.

Make a plan

Once you have the facts, you can make a plan for your retirement. Planning isn't easy. Many people enlist the help of a financial planning professional. This book will give you the basics. When you finish reading, you should:

- Understand the annuity options and other retirement resources available to you.

- Have a clear vision of your retirement goals, including the amount of income you'll need during retirement and the lifestyle you would like to enjoy.

- Be able to make sound choices about your retirement savings and benefits options.

- Avoid the big mistakes that can derail your retirement.

How to Work for Uncle Sam and Retire Rich will improve your knowledge of the federal retirement system. It will not, however, make you a financial planning professional. If you truly have the time and expertise to develop your own retirement plan, you should get to work! If you don't, you should interview some financial planners and find one with whom you will be comfortable working. The sooner you get started, the better.

How to use this book

This book is a plain English guide to government employee retirement benefits. Every chapter covers a topic of importance, and many chapters include worksheets designed to help you apply the concepts explained.

At the end of each chapter, you'll find a few review questions. Take time to answer them; they reinforce the key concepts presented in each chapter.

In between the chapters, you will find descriptions of some of the BIG mistakes federal government employees make when planning for retirement. At all costs, you should try to avoid making these mistakes.

The days when Uncle Sam provided a substantial retirement pension to all government workers are gone.

Chapter 1

The New Retirement and the "New" System

By the year 2016, 60.8 % of the federal non-seasonal full-time permanent workforce will be eligible to retire.[1] If you're one of them, I hope you've given your retirement more than a passing thought. For most government employees, the days when Uncle Sam provided a substantial retirement pension are gone. It's a fact that some federal government employees have not realized yet. If you wait until you retire to figure out exactly what Uncle Sam will provide, it may be too late to maximize your benefits, and it will certainly be too late to set aside savings to supplement the income you receive from the government.

Be honest with yourself. Have you really taken the time to sit down and talk with your spouse or significant other about your vision for retirement? Have you taken the time to figure out how much income you'll need to make that vision a reality? Have you estimated how much your government pension will provide? Do you know how much you should be saving each year to supplement your pension income so you can retire in comfort? If you haven't done most or even any of these things, you're not alone. Studies have found most Americans haven't taken time to plan properly for retirement.

As I write this, I hear my mother's voice in my head saying, "Just because everybody else is doing it doesn't mean you should." In this case, the saying should go "Just because nobody else is doing it doesn't mean you shouldn't!" You are responsible for your retirement. If you don't have a plan for reaching your goals, you need to step up to the plate and become proactive about

retirement. If you don't, you will almost certainly find yourself facing a retirement not meeting your expectations and lamenting the fact that you could have retired rich.

The ghost of retirement past:
The Civil Service Retirement System

If you have been working for the government since 1983 or earlier, it's likely you participate in the Civil Service Retirement System (CSRS). CSRS was introduced during the 1920s and provides retirement, disability, and survivor benefits to civilian employees. CSRS is generous—very generous. In return for contributing 7% of your pay to the program, you can generally expect to receive 55% to 65% of your "high-three" average salary.

For years, experts have been saying Americans need to save enough to provide 75% to 80% of their pre-retirement income during each year of retirement. If you're covered by CSRS, then you are on track to receive a significant portion of that amount without setting aside any additional savings at all. As a result, few CSRS participants feel any urgency to build substantial retirement savings accounts. If your home will be paid off, your children educated, and other big expenses will be behind you by the time you reach retirement, you may not feel the need to have additional savings.

Before you choose not to save, however, you should know this is a decision many people regret as retirement draws near. CSRS really only replaces 55% to 65% of income—not the 75% to 85% experts suggest. This means many CSRS participants have an income shortfall after they retire. If a hypothetical CSRS participant, Murray, is earning $60,000 a year when he retires, he will need about $48,000 during his first year of retirement. If his "high three" average salary is $60,000, CSRS will provide about $33,600 each year. That means Murray will need an additional $14,400 to supplement his pension income the first year. In later years, that amount will need to increase by the rate of inflation for Murray to maintain his lifestyle. (We'll talk more about inflation in a later chapter.) If he hasn't put aside any savings for retirement, he may have to change his lifestyle during retirement to accommodate his lower income. If Murray did set aside some savings, he'll need to determine how much income he can take each year without permanently depleting those savings.

How much of a retirement nest egg do you think Murray will need to provide himself with about $14,400 each year? If you want your savings to last throughout retirement, studies suggest you should withdraw *no more* than 5% from your savings and investments each year. So in our example, Murray needs at least $288,000 in personal savings to generate the $14,400 he needs each year to maintain his lifestyle after retirement. Of course, as an investor, he hopes to earn more than 5% on his investments so his nest egg will grow faster than inflation and allow him to increase his withdrawals over time.

Worksheet #1:
How much will you need to save to retire comfortably?

You can figure out how much you may need to save for retirement by completing this worksheet. Just review the example and fill in your own numbers to determine how much you'll need to save.

	Example:	Your numbers:
"High three" average salary	$60,000	_____
Income needed during retirement (Annual income x .80)	$48,800	_____
CSRS annuity	- $33,600[2]	_____
Additional income needed	= $ 14,400	_____
Savings needed (Additional income needed divided by .05)	$288.000	_____

The ghost of retirement present: The Federal Employees Retirement System

If you were hired in 1984 or later, it's likely you're covered by an entirely different federal pension program called the Federal Employees Retirement System (FERS). Toward the end of the 20th century, the federal government, and many corporations that sponsored defined benefit pension plans, realized the pension system had to change. With life expectancies lengthening rapidly, it simply became too expensive to maintain the current system.

Consequently, both the public and private sectors began to reformulate their retirement programs. Corporations introduced defined contribution plans, such as 401(k) plans, offering participants tax-advantaged ways to save. The federal government introduced FERS. The intent was to offer a plan that would compete effectively with the private sector, attracting the best and brightest minds to government service. At the same time, the government wanted to make it easier for employees who were moving from the public to the private sector, or vice-versa, to take their retirement benefits with them.

There are two basic parts to the FERS program: an annuity and Social Security benefits. In return for contributing 0.8% of your pay to FERS over 25-35 year's of employment, you generally can expect to receive 25% to 30% of your "high three" average salary in income during each year of your retirement. FERS participants also have 6.2% of their income withheld for Social Security taxes, which qualifies them to receive Social Security benefits after retirement. As a result, for 7% of their income, federal employees hired after December 31, 1983, who meet the eligibility requirements, will receive a FERS annuity and Social Security benefits.

CSRS versus FERS

Before rushing to judgment about whether CSRS or FERS is the better program, it's important to understand that legislation passed during the early 1980s required federal employees (with the exception of Congress) to begin participating in the Social Security System. Consequently, federal employees who participate in FERS contribute 6.2% of pay to Social Security and receive the same benefits as workers in the private sector who pay the same tax. CSRS participants do not have Social Security taxes withheld. As a result, CSRS employees do not receive Social Security benefits unless they also have employment in the private sector covered by Social Security.

The table below gives an example of the annuity income an employee with 30 years of service and a "high three" average salary of $60,000 might receive from each plan. Under CSRS, the yearly annuity payment is $33,600. Under FERS, the annuity payment is $18,000—a significant difference.

Understanding the differences between:	CSRS	FERS
Annual income	$60,000	$ 60,000
Retirement income needed (80% of pre-retirement income)	$48,000	$48,000
Annual annuity payment during retirement	$33,600[2]	$18,000[3]
Shortfall	$14,400	$30,000
Annual Social Security income	N/A	$14,388
Shortfall	$14,400	$15,612

As you can see, assuming Social Security benefits remain unchanged, a FERS participant may receive as much as $14,388 in Social Security income each year. When FERS and Social Security are combined, FERS participants receive an amount comparable to the income received by CSRS participants.

There are people for whom CSRS is the more attractive option, and there are people for whom FERS is the more attractive option. If you enjoy a high salary, CSRS may be the more beneficial program for you because Social Security benefits replace a smaller percentage of income for highly-compensated employees. If you are highly-compensated and qualify for FERS rather than CSRS, then you'll need to accumulate substantial personal savings if you want to preserve your current standard of living after retirement.

The Thrift Savings Plan

The Thrift Savings Plan (TSP) provides all federal employees—those who participate in CSRS and those who participate in FERS—with a tax-advantaged way to accumulate additional personal savings. The TSP, which was first introduced in 1987, is a tax-deferred retirement savings and investment plan, similar to a corporate 401(k) plan. The TSP puts you in control of your retirement savings.

- You decide how much to save, within plan and IRS limits.

- You decide how to invest those savings.

- Your contributions to the plan are made with pre-tax dollars, which may lower your current taxable income.

- Any earnings on the savings you invest grow tax-deferred until you begin to make withdrawals, generally after retirement.

- The government will match the contributions of FERS participants, up to 5% of their pay, allowing them to save more, faster.

Initially, few employees recognized the importance of setting aside personal savings to supplement their retirement income, and participation in the TSP was low. Many FERS participants were told by CSRS participants that their pensions would be more than adequate—testimony to the fact that few federal employees understood the differences between the two plans. FERS participants who did choose to participate were initially handicapped by the fact that the only investment option available was a Guaranteed Investment Contract offering a fairly low rate of return. Today, the TSP offers stock, bond, and government securities investment options so participants can choose to invest in a style consistent with their goals and risk tolerance.

If you are not currently enrolled in the TSP, you need to enroll ASAP! You can do so at any time. Just ask your personnel office for the TSP Election Form or download it from the TSP website at *www.tsp.gov*.

Ghost of retirement future:
It's never too late to save for retirement

Although public and private sector retirement programs are relatively comparable, the Employee Benefits Research Institute has found that people employed in the private sector are more aware of the need for personal retirement savings than those in the public sector. In addition, public sector employees are more likely to depend on pension income to fund retirement than those in the private sector.[4]

If you find yourself in retirement or approaching retirement without enough savings, there is no need for panic. However, there may be a need for flexibility. If you don't have enough retirement savings, you will need to make some choices—and they are not always easy choices. You can:

- **Retire later.** Give yourself more time to save by postponing your retirement. Working longer may increase the amount of your Social

Security benefits. It may also raise your "high three" average salary and increase the amount of your annuity income.

- **Live on less.** Choose a more frugal lifestyle after retirement instead of planning to maintain the lifestyle you enjoy today. If you have lower expectations, you may be able to live on less.

- **Save more.** Make sacrifices today so you save more and can enjoy greater comfort during retirement. Just a few dollars saved each week can make a big difference in the amount of savings you're able to set aside.

- **Work part-time.** More and more retirees are working after retirement. Some are working to provide higher levels of income; others are working because it gives them a sense of purpose.

Make a plan and stick with it

You need to begin saving and investing for your retirement. Don't save blindly, though. If you begin to save before you've set retirement goals and before you know how much you need to save, then you'll be providing yourself with a false sense of security. If you truly want to retire rich, you need to develop a plan for your retirement and stick with it. This means you need to understand the provisions of the retirement programs available to you and take full advantage of them. In the following chapters, you'll learn how to take control of your retirement by deciding what you want to accomplish; how much you need to save; where to invest your savings; and how to maximize the benefits available to you as a government employee.

Should you do it yourself?

Some people are very successful at planning, investing, and managing their wealth, while others are not. One of the obstacles individuals must overcome is the abundance of incomplete, inaccurate, and often sensationalized information about financial markets and investments received through electronic and print media. Professional guidance is invaluable when you're not sure what to believe, in part because an investment professional can help you maintain objectivity and avoid succumbing to emotion when making financial decisions.

CERTIFIED FINANCIAL PLANNERS™ spend years—even decades—mastering the art of developing and implementing coordinated strategies to help their clients accumulate wealth for the future. If you have the knowledge and are willing to spend your time developing, aligning, and managing financial strategies while at the same time keeping up with legislative and tax law changes, you may want to go it alone. If you don't, retaining the services of a professional financial planning team may be your best strategy.

Chapter Review

1. Are you covered by CSRS or FERS?

2. How much of your pre-retirement income will you need to live comfortably after retirement?

3. How much of your personal savings can you withdraw each year if your goal is to have your savings last throughout your retirement?

4. What are the tax advantages of the TSP?

5. If you don't have enough saved, and you are getting close to retirement, what are the four options available to you?

6. How should you plan for inflation?

Notes

[1] *An Analysis of Federal Employee Retirement Data.* United States Office of Personnel Management, Division of Strategic Human Resources Policy, Mar. 2008. Web. 28 Oct. 2009. <http://www.opm.gov/feddata/RetirementPaperFinal_v4.pdf>.

[2] *Retirement Facts 7: Computing Retirement Benefits Under the Civil Service Retirement System.* United States Office of Personnel Management. Web. 28 Oct. 2009. <http://www.opm.gov/Forms/pdfimage/RI83-7.pdf>.

[3] *FERS: Federal Employees Retirement System (An Overview of Your Benefits).* United States Office of Personnel Management. Web. 28 Oct. 2009. <http://www.opm.gov/forms/pdfimage/RI90-1.pdf>.

[4] *Issue Brief No. 292: Will More of Us Be Working Forever? The 2006 Retirement Confidence Survey.* Employee Benefit Research Institute, Apr. 2006. Web. 28 Oct. 2009. <http://www.ebri.org/pdf/briefspdf/EBRI_IB_04-20061.pdf>.

Big Mistake #1

Not understanding the effects of inflation and longer life expectancies

We are living longer. The average life expectancy for a 65 year old in 2003 was almost 78 years.[1] The good news is that we may enjoy longer retirements than our parents. The bad news is that we'll need more savings to ensure we enjoy them! As you decide how much to save for retirement, remember to factor in inflation. Inflation is the amount by which the cost of goods and services increases each year. As you can see in the table below, the prices of everyday goods can increase significantly over time.

The Effects of Inflation

	1996	2006
White bread	$ 0.86	$ 1.05
Ground chuck, 1 lb.	$ 1.80	$ 2.61
Navel oranges, 1 lb.	$ 0.56	$ 0.84
Eggs, Grade A, large, 1 doz.	$ 1.15	$ 1.45

Source: U.S. Department of Labor, Bureau of Labor Statistics

Your financial plan should incorporate inflation in two ways. First, you should plan to increase the amount you withdraw from your savings by about 3% each year, assuming inflation remains low. Second, you should keep a portion of your savings invested in growth investment options, such as stocks, that historically have provided returns that beat inflation and are higher than the returns provided by bonds and cash investments. You will want to carefully evaluate how much of your savings to invest in stocks, as they also have greater risks than other types of investments.

Note

[1] Hitti, Miranda. "U.S. Life Expectancy Best Ever, Says CDC." *WebMD*. WebMD, LLC, 28 Feb. 2005. Web. 28 Oct. 2009.
<http://www.webmd.com/news/20050228/us-life-expectancy-best-ever-says-cdc>.

*When you reach age 65, you'll either
have enough money saved to retire
comfortably—or you won't.*

Chapter 2
Getting Started

It's easy to talk about how much you plan to enjoy freedom from the constraints of a 9-to-5 workday. You may plan to spend time traveling, volunteering, starting a small business, or enjoying time with your family. Regardless of your dreams for retirement, you'll need to have financial resources, and accumulating wealth isn't easy. Ask yourself: How many truly wealthy people do I know?

During our youth, it seems as though we have plenty of time to build wealth before we retire so we often put off saving. As we get older, it becomes clear we should have saved while we were younger because accumulating wealth is a difficult challenge. It often gets more difficult with age because financial demands grow. You may buy a home. You may need to pay for college for your children. You may end up caring for elderly parents. The point is that you need to put away as much as you can as early as you can and do so within the context of a comprehensive financial plan.

The cost of procrastination

The longer you wait to begin saving, the more difficult wealth accumulation becomes. The following table shows how much you need to save each month if you want to have about $200,000 saved for retirement.

Age when savings begin:	Approximate monthly savings required:*
25	$57
35	$133
45	$338
55	$1,091

Source: *BankRate.com*

*This example assumes the investor has no current savings, will retire at age of 65, and earns an 8% average annual return.

It's never too late to put your financial house in order!

After spending decades helping people plan for the future, I am convinced that the vast majority of financial problems are behavioral in nature. People form poor money habits without even realizing they're doing it. Media and advertising encourage us to enjoy lavish lifestyles. Credit is readily available. It's far easier and more enjoyable to spend money than to save money. If you have lots of stuff and little money in the bank, you need to do some soul searching. In order to form sound money habits, you need to be willing to assess what's important to you, set goals, and pursue them. Often, that means giving up some of the unnecessary luxuries you may be enjoying.

It doesn't matter whether you are in your fifties, and feeling less prepared for retirement than you would like to be, or in your twenties and overwhelmed by the thought of managing your finances. There are simple steps you can take to make the process of accumulating wealth for retirement manageable.

1. Envision your retirement.

Talk with your spouse or significant other, if you have one, and make sure you're in agreement about the future. Be as specific as possible when you talk about what retirement will hold—don't generalize. It may be useful to write a description of your expectations for retirement so you can refer back to it. Here is a list of items to consider:

- Where will you live?

- What will a typical day in retirement be like?

- How much support would you like, or will you need, to provide to your children and/or your parents?

- Will you travel? If so, where and how?

- Will you work? Full or part-time?

- Will you do volunteer work? Where?

- What leisure activities will your pursue (golf, tennis, boating, etc.)?

- Will you provide care for your grandchildren?

- Will you have health coverage?

- Will you need life insurance?

A key factor to remember in modern retirement planning is that retirement today is vastly different than it was for past generations, and it will continue to evolve with advances in technology and health care. In the past, retirement was viewed as a period of fading activity, with a limited window of time to get one's affairs in order. But an increasing number of retirees in today's world are starting new businesses, indulging in hobbies, running marathons, and traveling around the world. They are essentially starting new "second" lives that begin once their primary careers are finished. Therefore, this may be a time for you to think about what you've always wanted to do in your life that was not possible before, like starting your own business or visiting far-off destinations.

As you envision your retirement, ask yourself what percentage of your pre-retirement income you'll need to sustain your standard of living after retirement. If 80% is enough, then you can set your savings goal at the level you calculated on Worksheet #1 in Chapter 1. If you'll need to replace a higher percentage of your pre-retirement income, you may want to reconsider that estimate. Once you know how much you'll need to save to provide additional income during retirement, set your contributions to the TSP at a level that will help you achieve your goal.

Remember that estimating your costs can be tricky because circumstances change over time. That's why it's a good idea to review the written description of your retirement expectations and revise it periodically.

2. Create a net worth statement.

A net worth statement is a handy tool for determining whether you are making progress toward your retirement goals. It can be as simple or as complex as you would like, from using a piece of notebook paper to employing financial software. What's important is that you list all of your assets and liabilities. Your net worth statement will provide you with a better understanding of where you are today.

Each year, update your net worth statement and compare it to the previous year's. (Tax time is a great time to do this.) As you make the comparison, ask yourself: Am I getting closer to my goal? If you are, you will feel wonderful. If you're not, you need to evaluate the cause. Are your savings growing? Are your investments performing? Are you accumulating more debt? Determine the problem and rectify it.

3. Understand the retirement options available to you.

Retirement under the federal system requires careful planning. It's essential that you understand and evaluate your options before you make any decision about when to retire. In the next chapter, we'll discuss the various retirement options available under CSRS and FERS, as well as eligibility requirements. The only way to determine a retirement date that allows you to maximize your annuity benefit is to understand the retirement benefits you may qualify to receive. If you make an uninformed decision, you could miss out on hundreds or even thousands of dollars in benefits.

The Office of Personnel Management website at *www.opm.gov* has retirement planning tools and calculators that can help you determine your retirement benefits.

When should you get started?

You should start planning and saving for retirement as soon as possible to ensure you'll have enough savings to maintain your standard of living after retirement. Begin by realistically envisioning your retirement and estimating how much you'll need to live comfortably. Establish a savings goal and begin contributing or increasing your contribution to the TSP. Develop a net worth

Worksheet #2:

Sample net worth statement   Date _____

What I own	What I owe
Personal Use Assets:	
Home _____	Mortgage _____
Other real estate or properties _____	Home equity loan _____
Automobiles _____	Car loans _____
Other vehicles _____	Student loans _____
Jewelry _____	Credit card debt _____
Collectibles _____	Real estate taxes _____
Furnishings _____	Income taxes _____
Investments: Stocks _____	Other _____
Bonds _____	Other _____
Mutual funds _____	Other _____
Exchange traded funds _____	Other _____
Money market accounts _____	Other _____
Annuities _____	Other _____
Retirement plan accounts (IRAs, TSP) _____	Other _____
Cash (Checking and savings accounts) _____	Other _____
Other _____	Other _____
Other _____	Other _____
Other _____	Other _____
Total assets: _____	**Total liabilities:** _____

My net worth (assets – liabilities) = _____

statement for yourself and update it each year to make sure you're making progress toward the goal. Finally, make sure you understand your retirement plan options.

Chapter Review

1. When should you begin planning for retirement?

2. How can a net worth statement help you prepare for retirement?

3. What are three steps you will take to get started planning for your retirement?

4. How much do you need to save each month to reach your retirement goals?

Big Mistake #2

Not having a comprehensive financial plan

When you build a home, you have a blueprint. When you start a business, you have a business plan. When you plan for your financial future, you need a comprehensive financial plan. Given the desirability of a comfortable and financially secure retirement, you would expect everyone to be motivated to develop such a plan. The unfortunate reality is that many households in the United States have never taken the time to develop plans for their financial future. In fact, some experts believe there is a direct correlation between the number of people declaring personal bankruptcy and the lack of personal financial planning in our country.

A quality financial plan must explore six core principles of the financial planning process:

- Cash management

- Risk management

- Tax strategies

- Investment planning

- Retirement planning

- Estate conservation

A competent professional can help you develop a comprehensive plan that capitalizes on your financial strengths and brings to light any weaknesses in your financial management. The key is finding an excellent planner. Look for professionals who have fulfilled the certification and renewal requirements of the Certified Financial Planner Board of Standards, Inc. These individuals have completed significant training and education and have earned the right to use the title CERTIFIED FINANCIAL PLANNER™ and the CFP® designation.

CSRS and FERS offer six retirement options.
Which will you qualify to take?

Chapter 3
Know Your Retirement Options

Have you ever walked into a coffee bar, looked up at the menu, and ordered something that wasn't exactly what you wanted because you just weren't sure what to choose? If you don't understand the difference between a latte, a cappuccino, a Café Americano, and an Espresso Macchiato, you're not alone. The good news is that you are pretty much guaranteed a jolt of caffeine no matter which option you select.

The government offers an array of retirement annuity options rivaling the drink options available at your local coffee house. You may qualify for voluntary retirement, voluntary early retirement, discontinued service retirement, special provision retirement, deferred retirement, and disability retirement. Each option is distinctly different, and each has unique eligibility requirements. A variety of factors will help determine the type of annuity you qualify to receive when you retire from government service. The most important factors are often your years of service and age, although the types of positions you hold within the government, your health, and the effect of any reorganizations on your position may also come into consideration. As with the coffee analogy, any annuity option will provide you with some retirement income. Your goal, however, is to get the most annuity income possible, so it's important for you to understand each of the options available as well as the corresponding eligibility requirements.

Voluntary retirement

You can take voluntary retirement from government service when you meet minimum age and service requirements. Under CSRS, you qualify for voluntary retirement at age 55 if you have 30 years of creditable service. Under FERS, you qualify at the minimum retirement age with at least 10 years of creditable service—which could be anywhere from age 55 to 57, depending on your date of birth. To receive an unreduced annuity at your minimum retirement age you will also need 30 years of creditable service. Under both CSRS and FERS, you may qualify for voluntary retirement at age 60 if you have 20 years of creditable service, or at age 62 if you have five years of creditable service.

Voluntary early retirement

If your agency undergoes a significant change in its personnel or work load, then it may request voluntary early retirement authority from the Office of Personnel Management (OPM). OPM determines whether the agency is undergoing a major reorganization, reduction in force, or transfer of function, and designates the specific geographic area(s) or occupation(s) covered by the retirement option. They also establish the period of time during which the early voluntary retirement option will be available to employees.

Discontinued service retirement

You may be eligible for a discontinued service retirement annuity if you are involuntarily separated from service (as long as you are not charged with misconduct or delinquency). If you do not meet the age and service requirements for voluntary retirement when separation occurs, you may qualify for discontinued service retirement if you are age 50 and have 20 years of creditable service. If you have 25 years of creditable service, including 5 years of civilian service, you may choose this type of retirement at any age.

Special provision retirement

Law enforcement officers, firefighters, and air traffic controllers are covered by special retirement provisions because of the physical demands of their jobs. The special provision annuity is calculated using a more

liberal annuity formula making voluntary retirement—at an earlier age than normal—economically feasible.

Deferred retirement

If you resign with fewer than five years of government service, you do not qualify for retirement benefits unless you return to government service during your career. If you are covered by CSRS or FERS and have more than five years of civilian service, but resign before you meet the age and service requirements needed to receive immediate benefits, you may collect a deferred annuity. Your benefit will be determined based on your "high three" average salary and your length of service.

Note: In order to be eligible to continue with FEHB health insurance benefits and/or FEGLI life insurance benefits, you must retire with an immediate annuity

Disability retirement

To qualify for disability retirement under either CSRS or FERS, you must be unable to perform your *current* job and be willing to accept a suitable position within your agency. The position must be within your commuting area and at the same grade or pay level as your current position. This is a more generous definition of disability than that of Social Security, which requires that you be unable to perform any job, not just your current job. So you may qualify for CSRS or FERS disability even if you don't qualify for Social Security disability payments.

Note: To be eligible for disability retirement benefits under FERS, you must apply for Social Security disability benefits.

Eligibility requirements

Each of the available retirement options has specific eligibility requirements. In general, your eligibility will depend on:

- Your total years of creditable service (You should verify that your retirement service computation date is correct.)

- The age at which you become eligible to retire

CSRS Table: Eligibility requirements by type of annuity

Type of Retirement	Age	Years of Service Required	Special Requirements	Other Considerations
Voluntary	62	5		
	60	20	None	Must meet the 1-out-of-2 requirement
	55	30		
Early Optional (Voluntary Separation) Reduction for Age	Any Age	25	Your agency must undergo a major reorganization, transfer of function, or reduction in force, as determined by OPM. OPM must grant your agency authority to administer an early out.	Age reduction is equal to 1/6 of 1% for each full month the employee is younger than age 66 (2% per year). The age reduction is permanent.
	50	20		
Discontinued Service Retirement (Involuntary Separation) Reduction for Age	Any Age	25	You must not decline any reasonable offer of a position. Your separation must not be for misconduct or delinquency.	Age reduction is equal to 1/6 of 1% for each full month the employee is younger than age 55 (2% per year). The age reduction is permanent.
	50	20		
Special Provision Retirements (Law Enforcement Officers and Firefighters)	50	20 years qualifying service	You must serve in a primary position and transfer directly to a secondary position without a break in service exceeding three days.	Mandatory retirement age is 57 for law enforcement officers and firefighters.
Special Provision Retirements (Air Traffic Controllers)	50	20 years qualifying service	None	Subject to mandatory separation at age 56 even if the employee does not have sufficient years of ATC service.
	Any Age	25 years qualifying service		
Disability	Any Age	5	Disabled for current position and any vacant position at same grade and pay level within commuting area of your agency.[1]	1-out-of-2 requirement does not apply.
Deferred	62	5	Must have left retirement contributions in fund.	Must meet the 1-out-of-2 requirement.

Footnotes

[1] Your application must be made prior to retirement, or within one year of separation, unless you are mentally incompetent.

FERS Table: Eligibility requirements by type of annuity

Types of Retirement	Age	Years of Service Req'd	Special Requirements	Other Considerations
Voluntary (No Age Reduction)	MRA	30	None	
	60	20		None
	62	5		
MRA + 10 (Voluntary) Age Reduction	MRA	10	None	Annuity will be reduced by 5/12 of 1% for each full month the employee is younger than age 62 (5% per year).[1]
Early Optional (Voluntary)	50	20	To qualify for early out, your agency must undergo a major reorganization, transfer of function, or reduction in force, as determined by OPM. OPM must grant authority to administer an early out.	Under FERS, there is no age reduction for being younger than age 55 at retirement.[2]
	Any Age	25		
Discontinued Service (Involuntary)	50	20	You must not decline any reasonable offer of a position. Your separation must not be for misconduct or delinquency.	Under FERS, there is no age reduction for being younger than age 55 at retirement.
	Any Age	25		
Special Provision Retirements (Law Enforcement Officer, Firefighter)	50	20 years qualifying service	Must complete 3 years in primary (first-line) position before moving to a secondary position without a break in service.	Mandatory retirement at age 57 for law enforcement officers and firefighters.
	Any Age	25 years qualifying service		
Special Provision Retirements (Air Traffic Controllers)	50	20	None	Mandatory retirement is at age 56, or upon completion of 20 years of service under special provisions.
	Any Age	25		

Footnotes

[1] Under the MRA + 10 Provision, an employee can elect to postpone the start date of the annuity to reduce or eliminate the age reduction.

[2] A FERS retiree who has a portion of his or her annuity subject to CSRS rules will have the 2% age reduction applied to the CSRS component, if they are younger than age 55.

In addition, your eligibility will be determined by the system in which you participate.

CSRS retirement options

If you are covered by a CSRS annuity, you must meet two minimum eligibility requirements:

1. You must have *five years of civilian service*.

2. You must meet the *1-out-of-2 requirement*, which means you must be in a covered position on your date of separation for one of the last two years prior to separating for retirement. (If retirement is based on disability, the 1-out-of-2 rule is waived, but you must be covered by CSRS when you become disabled.)

In addition to these broad minimum requirements, each retirement annuity available through CSRS is guided by specific age and service rules. You'll find these requirements in the CSRS table.

FERS retirement options

If you are covered by a FERS annuity, you also have minimum eligibility requirements:

1. You must have *five years of civilian service*.

2. You must be serving in a position covered under FERS at retirement.

The age and service requirements for FERS are described in the FERS table.

Determining your retirement date under CSRS

As you can see in the tables, CSRS allows you to retire voluntarily at age 55, as long as you have 30 years of service. It is important to understand you must meet both age *and* service requirements when determining your retirement date. For both CSRS and FERS employees, your retirement eligibility is determined using your age on the day before your birthday.

Example: Determining a retirement date for a CSRS employee

John was born on August 21, 1951. He is retiring under CSRS, and his service computation date for retirement is February 13, 1973. When is John's earliest optional retirement opportunity under CSRS?

8/21/55	Date of birth
+ 55	Earliest age for retirement eligibility
8/20/2011	**Date John is considered to have reached age 55**
2/13/78	Service Computation Date
+ 30	Years of service needed at age 55
2/13/2008	**Date John acquires 30 years of service**

John attains the age *and* service requirements needed to retire voluntarily on August 20, 2011.

Determining your retirement date under FERS

If you are covered by FERS, your minimum retirement age is determined by the year in which you were born. If you were born before 1948, you can retire at age 55. If you were born in 1948 or later, your retirement age gradually increases to age 57, as you can see in the FERS Minimum Requirement Age Table.

FERS Minimum Requirement Age Table

If you were born:	Your minimum requirement age is:
Before 1948	55
In 1948	55 and 2 months
In 1949	55 and 4 months
In 1950	55 and 6 months
In 1951	55 and 8 months
In 1952	55 and 10 months
From 1953 to 1964	56
In 1965	56 and 2 months
In 1966	56 and 4 months
In 1967	56 and 6 months
In 1968	56 and 8 months
In 1969	56 and 10 months
1970 and after	57

To receive an unreduced annuity at your minimum requirement age, you must have 30 years of service; however, you may retire with as little as 10 years of

service (5 years must be civilian service) and receive a reduced annuity. Your annuity is reduced by 5% per year (five-twelfths per month) for each year that you are under age 62 when you retire. If you retire under the MRA + 10 retirement provision, you can choose to postpone the start date of your annuity to reduce or eliminate the age reduction, and—if you postpone receiving your annuity until age 62—you will not receive an age reduction.

Example: Determining a retirement date for a FERS employee

Mary was born on May 4, 1965. She is retiring under FERS, and her service computation date for retirement is June 20, 1988. When is her earliest optional retirement opportunity with no age reduction under FERS?

5/04/65	Date of birth
+ 56 & 2 months	Minimum retirement age – born in 1965
7/3/2021	**Date Mary reaches her MRA**
6/20/88	Service Computation Date
+ 30	Years of service needed at MRA
6/20/2018	**Date Mary acquires 30 years of service**

Mary attains the age and service requirements to retire voluntarily with no age reduction on July 3, 2021.

Forms and documentation

The retirement application process requires documentation. You are responsible for completing some of the forms, and your agency is responsible for completing others. It's important to begin the process of applying for your retirement annuity early so that you and your agency both have time to complete the appropriate paperwork. You can find a list of forms, as well as instructional material, on the OPM Web site at *www.opm.gov*.

Chapter Review

1. Name two factors that will help determine your eligibility for retirement.

2. Name three of the six types of retirement annuities available.

3. When might you have to take a reduced retirement annuity?

Big Mistake #3

Not having an estate plan

The persistent rumor that someday you will die is true. In preparation for this event, it is essential to create and maintain an effective estate plan. An estate plan benefits both you and your loved ones in the event of your incapacity and upon your death. Planning now, while you are healthy, enables you to choose appropriate fiduciaries to handle your affairs. Without such a plan in place, the court will appoint a conservator if you are incapacitated and will appoint an administrator upon your death. The court will also appoint guardians for your minor children.

By taking the time to plan now, you make these decisions yourself instead of leaving it up to the court. Moreover, you choose your beneficiaries instead of having the state determine them for you; you are able to plan the manner and timing of distributions to those beneficiaries; and you can avoid probate and minimize taxes. Thus estate planning has lasting benefits for both you and your loved ones. The documents most commonly used in estate planning, both basic and advanced, are described below.

Basic estate planning

Generally, the documents comprising a basic estate plan are a revocable living trust, a pour over will, an advance health care directive or health care power of attorney and living will, a durable power of attorney for financial matters, and a Health Insurance Portability and Accountability Act authorization.

Revocable Living Trust. People often use a revocable living trust to avoid probate, implement tax planning strategies, and to control the manner and timing of distributions to beneficiaries. Unlike a will, which is a public document filed with the court, the trust is private. Property held in the name of the trust is not subject to probate proceedings.

You need to transfer your assets (e.g., real estate) into the trust, generally with the assistance of an attorney. You continue to control and manage the assets as you do now, but upon your incapacity, your named successor trustee manages

the trust assets on your behalf without a court having to appoint a conservator. Upon your death, your successor trustee distributes the assets to your beneficiaries according to the terms of the trust.

Will. A "pour over" will is typically used in conjunction with a living trust to catch any assets that may not have been transferred to the trust during your lifetime so they can be distributed according to the trust's terms. You also nominate guardians for your minor children in the will.

Durable Power of Attorney for Financial Matters. A Durable Power of Attorney for property management enables a designated individual to handle your non-trust assets (e.g., pay your bills from a non-trust checking account, transfer assets to your living trust) in the event you are incapacitated.

Advance Health Care Directive, Power of Attorney for Health Care, and Living Will. An Advance Health Care Directive or Power of Attorney for Health Care allows you to designate an agent to make health care decisions for you in the event you are incapacitated. In addition to the release and execution of health care records and forms and consent to surgery and the like, it can be used to express your preferences regarding life-sustaining care. In some states, you express your directives to medical providers and medical institutions in a Living Will.

Health Insurance Portability and Accountability Act Authorization. A Health Insurance Portability and Accountability Act ("HIPAA") authorization permits your designated agent to obtain protected medical information about you in order to handle your medical affairs.

Advanced estate planning

Larger estates—those in excess of the federal estate tax credit amount or applicable exclusion amount ($3.5 million in 2009)—may benefit from one or more of the following strategies and associated documents, which can be used alone or in conjunction with others.

Irrevocable Life Insurance Trust. There is a common misconception that life insurance proceeds are not subject to federal estate tax. While the proceeds are free from income tax, they are included as part of your taxable estate and, therefore, significant value can be lost to estate taxes. An Irrevocable Life Insurance Trust (ILIT) is created specifically for the purpose of owning your life

insurance policy. The ILIT holds the policy outside of your estate and shelters the proceeds from estate tax. The proceeds can then be used to provide your estate with the liquidity to pay estate taxes, pay off debts, pay final expenses, and provide income to a surviving spouse or children. You can use your annual gift tax exclusion to make cash gifts to your ILIT to pay the premiums on the life insurance policy.

Qualified Personal Residence Trust. A Qualified Personal Residence Trust (QPRT) allows you to gift your house or vacation home at a discount, freeze its value for estate tax purposes, and still continue to live in it.

Family Limited Partnerships and Limited Liability Companies. Family Limited Partnerships (FLPs) and Limited Liability Companies (LLCs) are entities involving members of your family. The main advantages of forming and funding FLPs and LLCs involve estate and gift tax savings and asset protection.

Grantor Retained Trusts. A Grantor Retained Annuity Trust (GRAT) is an irrevocable trust to which you contribute assets. You retain the right to receive annuity payments for a specified period of time based on an assumed discount rate determined by the IRS. At the end of the term, assets in the trust pass to other beneficiaries. The GRAT provides gift and estate tax savings if the return on the assets placed in the GRAT exceeds the assumed discount rate. Grantor Retained Unitrusts (GRUTs), where distributions are based on a percentage of assets instead of an annuity, and Grantor Retained Interest Trusts (GRITs), where you retain an income interest, are similar techniques.

Intentionally Defective Grantor Trusts. Alternatively, you may want to sell assets to an Intentionally Defective Grantor Trust (IDGT), an irrevocable trust you establish that is excluded from your estate for federal estate tax purposes, yet owned by you for income tax purposes. The sale can be in exchange for a promissory note. Similar to a GRAT, the sale of the promissory note provides gift and estate tax savings if the return on the IDGT exceeds the interest rate on the note.

Charitable Planning Documents. If you are charitably inclined and seek to minimize taxes while enhancing the amounts going to your loved ones, you may want to consider charitable planning. Documents associated with charitable planning include Charitable Remainder Trusts (CRATs and CRUTs), Charitable Lead Trusts (CLATs and CLUTs), and Private Foundations.

In preparing any of the foregoing documents, it is important to work with a qualified attorney because the law in this area is very specialized, changes often, and involves complex tax matters. The ramifications for you and your loved ones can be far-reaching, both emotionally and financially.

*It's essential to estimate the amount of income
your annuity will actually provide.*

Chapter 4
Key Decisions and Numbers

Get your calculators out! You've envisioned your retirement, evaluated your current financial position, and understand your annuity's eligibility rules. You have a preliminary estimate of the amount of income you'll need to live comfortably during retirement. Now you need to estimate how much income your annuity will actually provide.

This exercise requires a certain amount of patience and willingness to do some simple mathematics, but don't worry. For those of you who avoid numbers and any situations requiring mathematical calculations, there is software available to help! If you prefer to avoid computers, too, you can opt to work with a financial planning professional who can help you crunch the numbers. It's worth it. After all, you wouldn't want to leave hundreds or thousands of dollars on the table just because you aren't comfortable with math—especially when your goal is to retire rich.

A retirement income review

While it's fairly easy to estimate the amount of income you'll need to live comfortably during retirement, that amount is a moving target. There are at least three factors that can significantly affect your income needs—and two of them cannot be predicted with certainty. The components are life expectancy, the level of income you'll be earning at retirement, and inflation.

Life expectancy

None of us knows how long we'll live once we retire; however, life expectancies are increasing rapidly. The average 65-year-old can expect to live almost 20 more years. Of course, genetics will play a role in your longevity, too. No matter what your family history is like, my advice is to not underestimate your life expectancy. I know I would rather live comfortably throughout a long retirement than run out of money and become a burden to my family. I can always provide my heirs and favorite charities with an attractive inheritance.

Salary changes

Determining how much you'll need to live comfortably after retirement is a challenge because the amount is tricky. It's likely that each time you receive an increase in pay you also increase your standard of living. You may buy nicer cars, move into a bigger house, or just enjoy a few more indulgences. Maybe you spend that extra money paying for college for your children. Perhaps you buy a second home. Whenever you increase your standard of living, you need to increase your estimate of the amount you will need for retirement. Consequently, you'll need to review your retirement plan as often as your income changes.

Inflation

If you can, it would be wise to take a significant portion of any increase in income and use it to build your retirement savings. Why? Because the third challenge in determining how much you'll need after retirement is inflation. Inflation is the annual increase in the cost of goods and services we buy every day. It can translate into a lot of money over time—just ask older relatives whether they paid more for their first house or their last car.

When you think about inflation, consider the cost of a postage stamp. During the past 30 years or so, the cost of a first class stamp in the United States has increased from 10 cents to 44 cents. Imagine that—an increase in cost of 312%. No, stamps have not increased at a rate faster than the rate of inflation. In fact, they have increased in cost slightly slower than inflation, as measured by the Consumer Price Index. If they had kept pace with inflation, a first class stamp

would have cost 42 cents back in 2005. Estimating the impact of inflation is tricky. You'll find some costs increase slower than inflation, while others increase faster than inflation.

Understanding inflation

Year	Cost of a stamp
1974	$ 0.10
1988	$ 0.24
1995	$ 0.32
2002	$ 0.37
2006	$ 0.39
2008	$ 0.42

Source: Postal Rate Commission

One thing is certain, however. Inflation will affect your retirement income—before *and* after you retire. You need to factor in inflation for every year up to and throughout your retirement. Unfortunately, inflation isn't easy to predict. During the 1930s, America experienced deflation and prices actually fell. During the 1970s, inflation averaged more than 7% each year. When you factor inflation into your calculations, I suggest you use an historical average. Over the long term, from 1913 through current times, inflation has averaged about 3.5% each year.[1]

Example 1: The Power of Inflation

John, age 45, earns $40,000 each year. He plans to retire in 20 years and estimates he'll live for 30 years in retirement. He plans to spend 90% of his pre-retirement income during each year of retirement and estimates inflation will be 3.5% on average each year. After adjusting for inflation, John should plan to spend $71,632 during his first year of retirement and $201,057 in his last.

Replacement retirement income

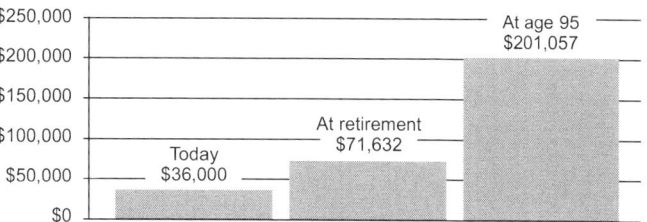

Source: Financial Calculators (http://www.fincalc.com/)

You may find the example a bit shocking. Many people are surprised by the power of inflation. Don't let these figures overwhelm you, though. It's important to remember John will probably see his income rise along with inflation during the 20 years before his retirement. In addition, there is a not-so-secret weapon that can help your savings keep pace with or even surpass inflation. It's called compound interest.

Compound interest

It has been said that Einstein called compound interest the eighth wonder of the world. Compounding happens when you invest and your investment earns interest or capital gains. If you reinvest the interest and capital gains, they have an opportunity to earn more interest and capital gains, and so on. Compound interest can help you battle inflation over time.

For example, imagine you put $10,000 into an investment that returns 7% each year, and your interest compounds monthly. The following table shows the value of your investment over a variety of periods. As you can see, the growth is significant. Imagine what it would be like if you continued to add to the account over time.

Number of years	Approximate value of account
5 years	$14,176
10 Years	$20,097
20 years	$40,387
30 years	$ 81,165
40 years	$163,114
50 years	$327,804

Compounding interest over time is like a snowball rolling down a hill. The longer the hill, the larger the snowball can become. Compounding is an important tool in the fight against inflation.

Calculating the value of your annuity

Will your annuity provide you with the income you need to retire rich? The only way to know is to crunch some numbers and figure out how much you'll receive each year. The amount of your annuity will depend on your length of creditable service and "high-three" average salary, as well as options, adjustments, voluntary contributions, or special provisions that may affect you.

Creditable service

In Chapter 2, we discussed the fact that creditable service can significantly affect the amount of your retirement annuity. Therefore, it's important to check with your Personnel Office periodically to ensure your Official Personnel Folder (OPF) contains all your creditable service—civilian and military. Be careful not to overestimate creditable service in your own calculations by counting seasonal work completed during a particular year as a full year of service. Unused sick leave can extend your length of service if you qualify for CSRS benefits or FERS benefits when there is a CSRS component. Creditable service also includes:

- The amount of time between dates of appointment and separation

- Leave without pay for up to six months in a calendar year

- Workers' compensation time, as long as you return to service within the required time frame

- Part-time service (The rules are different for CSRS and FERS participants.)

- Intermittent service for actual days or hours worked

- Breaks in service of up to three days

If your retirement is approaching, request your annuity estimate as soon as possible. In some cases, it can take as long as 90 days before you receive the information you need.

Creditable Civilian Service Table—CSRS Annuity

This table provides an example of a length of service computation for a *CSRS retiree.* In the example, the annuity is based on 32 years and 9 months of service because only full years and months are considered in the calculation.

Type of Service:	Number of Years	Number of Months	Number of Days
Civilian	28	1	3
Military	4	2	6
Unused Sick Leave	0	6	18
Total Service	**32 years**	**9 months**	**27 days**

Your "high-three" average salary

Your annuity benefits are expressed as a percentage of your "high-three" average salary. Your "high-three" average salary is the average of your basic pay during the three consecutive years your earnings were highest. For average salary purposes, your basic pay includes:

- Night differential pay for wage grade employees

- Environmental differential pay

- Locality pay

- Premium pay for stand-by time, which primarily affects firefighters

- Premium pay for irregular administratively uncontrolled overtime (AUO)

- Law enforcement availability pay (LEAP) (also known as "premium pay")

Some types of compensation are not included in "high-three" calculations. These include:

- Cash awards and bonuses

- Overtime pay, with some exceptions

- Military pay

- Holiday pay

- Travel pay outside of the regular tour of duty

- Any other special allowances

Most people will rely on the Office of Personnel Management to provide an accurate measure of their "high-three" average salary.

Your CSRS annuity

The amount of your CSRS annuity is determined using a three-part formula based on your length of creditable service. The CSRS annuity formula provides:

> *1.50% per year for the first five years (or 7.5%)*

> *1.75% per year for the next five years (or 8.75%)*

> *2.00% per year for service of greater than 10 years*

After 10 years of service, your annuity will be 16.25% of your "high-three" average salary. After 30 years, your annuity will be 56.25% of your "high-three." By law, the maximum annuity is 80% of your "high-three". You can, however, include creditable, unused sick leave to increase the amount of your annuity.

.

Worksheet #1:
How much will your CSRS annuity provide?
Review the example and fill in your own numbers

	Example:			*Your numbers:*		
"High three" average salary:	$47,000			_____		
	Year	*Month*	*Date*	*Year*	*Month*	*Date*
Retirement date:	2013	12	31	_____		
Service computation date:	1981	2	13	_____		
Total service equals:	**32 years**	**10 months**	**19 days**	_____		
Add unused sick leave:		0				
Subtract non-creditable service:		0		_____		
Total computation years:		*32 years 10 months*		_____		

Basic annuity computation:

1.50% x $47,000 x 5 years = $3,525.00	_____
1.75% x $47,000 x 5 years = $4,115.00	_____
2.00% x $47,000 x 22$^{10}/_{12}$ years = $21,463.33	_____
Total basic annual annuity: $29,100.83	_____

CSRS offset benefits

If you were lucky enough to work for the government before the Social Security Amendment of 1983, you may receive a very generous CSRS Offset annuity benefit. The Social Security amendment requires that all employees hired by the Federal Government after December 31, 1983, participate in the Social Security system. The law also applies to former federal employees who were covered by CSRS before they were rehired—on or after December 31, 1983—if their breaks

in service were longer than 365 days. These employees are known as CSRS Offset employees. You are a CSRS Offset employee if you meet the following three requirements:

- Had 5 or more years of creditable civilian service as of December 31, 1986,

- Had a break in federal service longer than 365 days, and

- Were rehired following a break in service after December 31, 1983.

If you had a break in service after December 31, 1986, you only qualify for offset benefits if you had five years of creditable service as of the date of the break. Offset employees pay 0.8% of contributions to the CSRS fund, and 6.2% to the Social Security Administration. If you earn more than the maximum Social Security wage base, your CSRS salary deductions will be 7%.

Computing CSRS offset benefits

CSRS Offset employees are entitled to the same retirement benefits as other CSRS employees until they reach age 62. Then they need to recalculate their benefits, and they often end up with more income than they had before age 62.

At age 62, your offset benefits are reduced by the amount of your Social Security benefits (if you are eligible for Social Security benefits). The offset, or reduction, in your CSRS annuity will equal the lesser of:

- The amount of the Social Security benefit credited to your CSRS offset service since December 31, 1983, or

- The amount obtained by dividing your total years of CSRS offset service by 40, and then multiplying the result by your total Social Security Benefit.

The amount of the reduction in your CSRS annuity will generally be less than the amount of the Social Security benefit you will begin to receive, resulting in a net increase in your income.

Example 2: CSRS Offset Computation

Marie Smith retires at age 55 with 30 years of federal service. Of these years, 15 were completed after 1983. This is Marie's offset service. She also spent 10 years in the private sector and was covered by Social Security during that time.

Computation at Retirement (age 55):

High-three average salary:	$30,000
Total computation years:	30 years

Annuity computation:

1.50% x $47,000 x 5 = $2,250.00
1.75% x $47,000 x 5 = $2,625.00
2.00% x $47,000 x 20 = $12,000.00
Total annual annuity: $16,875.00

Computation at age 62:

Total Social Security benefit:	$ 9,600 per year
Social security credited to CSRS Offset years	$ 6,600 per year
Years of offset service:	15 years

Option 1:	$ 6,600
Option 2: (15 years/40 X $9,600)	$ 3,600
Value of CSRS annuity:	$16,875
Minus lesser amount:	$ 3,600
New annuity amount:	$13,275

Benefits at age 62:

CSRS annuity:	$13,275
Social Security benefits:	$ 9,600

Total benefits:	**$22,875 annually**

Your FERS annuity

As you know, the benefits provided by FERS annuities are not as high as those provided by CSRS. However, if you have a FERS annuity, you will also qualify to receive Social Security benefits. The amount of your FERS annuity also will depend on your "high-three" average salary and length of creditable service. The FERS annuity formula pays:

> *Retirement before age 62:* 1% of your "high-three" average salary times your years of creditable service.

> *Retirement after age 62:* 1.1% of your "high-three" average salary times your years of creditable service.

If you retire at age 55 with 30 years of service, your annual annuity will be 30% of your "high-three" pay. Retiring at age 62 with 30 years of service will provide 33% of your "high-three" pay.

FERS annuity supplement

Employees with at least one calendar year (a calendar year is from January 1 to December 31) of FERS service are eligible for a Special Retirement Supplement. The Special Retirement Supplement (also known as the FERS annuity supplement) is a benefit for those who retire:

- After 30 years of service, at the minimum retirement age,

- After 20 years of service, at age 60, or

- Under discontinued service or early voluntary retirement provisions. (These employees do not begin to receive the Special Retirement Supplement until they reach the minimum retirement age.)

The amount of the supplement is approximately equal to the Social Security benefit you earned while you were employed by the government. If your earnings during retirement exceed the amount exempted by Social Security, your supplement may be reduced or eliminated.

Worksheet #2:
How much will your FERS annuity provide?

Review the example and fill in your own numbers

	Example:			Your numbers:		
"High three" average salary:	$47,000					
Age:	55 years old					
	Year	Month	Date	Year	Month	Date
Retirement date:	2013	12	31			
Service computation date:	1981	2	13			
Total service equals:	**32 years**	**10 months**	**19 days**			
Add unused sick leave*:	0					
Subtract non-creditable service:	0					
Total computation years:	32 years	10 months				

Basic annuity computation: $1.00\% \times \$47,000 \times 37^{10}/_{12} \text{ years} = \$15,431.67$

* President Obama recently signed the National Defense Authorization Act that allows credit for sick leave in the computation of FERS annuities. This new benefit is a phase-in starting in 2010. FERS employees retiring before December 31, 2013, will receive a 50% credit for unused sick leave; after January 1, 2014, they will receive full credit for unused sick leave.

Options and adjustments

Once your basic annual annuity has been determined under CSRS or FERS, then you'll need to factor in any reductions or additions that may apply. Your retirement annuity could be reduced for early retirement, civilian or military service credit unpaid deposits, unpaid re-deposits or survivor benefit reductions.

Voluntary contributions

If you want to retire really rich, you should consider making voluntary contributions to supplement your retirement. CSRS and CSRS Offset employees

have an opportunity to open voluntary contribution accounts in the Civil Service Trust Fund. You invest after-tax dollars and earn tax-deferred interest. Voluntary contributions are made in addition to your required CSRS or CSRS Offset and Social Security contributions.

When you are ready, you can choose to withdraw the funds in a lump sum, receive the funds through a lifetime annuity to supplement your CSRS or CSRS Offset annuity, or transfer the funds to another retirement account like an Individual Retirement Account (IRA). If you don't withdraw or transfer the money out of your voluntary contribution account, the Office of Personnel Management will assume you would like it to increase your CSRS annuity benefit.

If your voluntary contributions are used for a supplemental annuity, you'll receive a $7 increase in your annual CSRS retirement benefit for every $100 invested. You'll also receive an extra annuity benefit of 20 cents for every year past age 55, if you choose to retire later. For example, if you retire at age 60, your voluntary contributions will increase your annuity by $8 instead of $7 per $100 invested each year. The extra dollar is 20 cents times five years.

You can also elect to provide a survivor benefit for a loved one, which will reduce the amount of your voluntary contribution annuity. He or she will receive 50% of your reduced voluntary contribution benefit. Voluntary contribution annuities are not adjusted for inflation.

Special provisions

If you served as an air traffic controller, military reservist technician, law enforcement officer, or firefighter, your annuity is subject to the special provisions reviewed in the last chapter.

Your retirement

If you will be retiring within the next few years, you should plan to request a benefits estimate at least six months prior to your anticipated retirement date. You can also enlist the services of a Certified Financial Planner® practitioner who specializes in federal employee benefits.

Chapter Review

1. Which of the following is used to compute your annual annuity?

    a. Creditable service hours

    b. "High-three" average salary

    c. Unused sick leave

    d. All of the above

2. To calculate your "high-three" average salary, you just total your basic pay during the three consecutive years you earned the most, and then divide that amount by three.

    a. True

    b. False

3. How are the CSRS annuity and the CSRS Offset annuity different?

4. Name two tools that can help your savings and income keep pace with inflation.

5. If you're not comfortable computing your annuity, what are two options available to you?

Notes

[1] *InflationData.com.* Financial Trend Forecaster(R). Web. 28 Oct. 2009. <http://inflationdata.com/inflation/>.

Big Mistake #4

Purchasing a fixed income annuity option

Earlier in this chapter, you learned about the dramatic effects of inflation. Remember the postage stamp? One of the annuity options offered to participants in the TSP is a life income option. It is a fixed annuity. The good news is that it provides you with income during your lifetime (and that of your spouse, if you choose the survivorship option). The bad news is that the amount you receive is always the same. It will never increase, so as inflation goes up, your purchasing power will go down. You'll be able to buy less even though you have the same income.

There are some other drawbacks to a fixed income annuity. If you don't live long enough to draw down all of the income in your account, any remainder is forfeited. One course of action is to select a survivorship option. When you choose a survivorship option, your spouse will also receive level payments of a reduced amount until his or her death, and then the payments will stop.

If you choose to annuitize your TSP account, I would encourage you to investigate a systematic withdrawal method allowing you to periodically increase the amount you receive. This allows you to increase your income as inflation increases.

The best option for many people is to roll over their TSP accounts into IRAs. They'll have additional investment options, any earnings will continue to grow tax deferred, and they'll have the opportunity to withdraw as much or as little as they need each year. Contact an investment professional who is capable of helping you make the right decisions about how to manage the savings in your TSP account.

Do you really want to retire rich?
Join the TSP.

Understanding the Thrift Savings Plan

It's easy to say you want to retire rich. It's more difficult to take the actions needed to make it happen. For example, given a choice:

- Will you save $1,000 this year or take a nicer vacation?

- Would you prefer to tuck away several hundred dollars each month or make payments on a sporty car or a fishing boat?

- Will you save one-half of your pay raise or splurge on a bigger house?

This is the choice: Do you choose greater enjoyment today or delay gratification so that you can also enjoy the future? It's a decision you need to make. If you make the right one, you can retire rich. If you're smart you can make some good choices today and let compound interest do most of the work for you.

The advantage of saving early

Prahni starts saving and investing in the TSP at age 25. He saves for just 10 years. Michelle waits and starts saving at age 35. She saves every year for the next 30 years, but she will still have less at retirement than Prahni does. Starting early can make a big difference.

The Effects of Inflation

	Prahni	Michelle
Age (while saving)	25-35 (10 years)	35-65 (30 years)
Monthly contribution	$100	$100
Total amount of contributions	$12,000	$36,000
Average annual return (Compounded monthly)	8%	8%
Approximate account balance at age 65	**$202,500**	**$150,100**

Retiring rich isn't impossible—even if you don't make a huge salary. Anyone can do it. You simply have to spend less today and save more for tomorrow. For some people, this may be a more difficult challenge than for others. If you *really* want to retire rich, it's a choice you have to make. And the sooner you make it, the richer you can retire.

What is a Thrift Savings Plan?

The TSP is a secret weapon for government employees who want to retire rich. While CSRS, FERS, and Social Security are defined benefit plans—that is, they pay a specific benefit after retirement and the only way to increase that benefit is to work longer or retire later—the Thrift Savings Plan (TSP) is a defined contribution plan. That means the TSP defines the amount you can contribute, but your benefits after retirement are limited only by the amount of your contributions and the earnings on your contributions. You can save as much or as little as you choose, within IRS limits. This means you can build substantial savings that will help you retire with more than enough income to live comfortably.

The TSP is administered by the Federal Retirement Thrift Investment Board. In many ways, it's similar to a corporate 401(k) plan. FERS and CSRS employees—both full and part time—are eligible to contribute either a percentage of basic pay or a fixed dollar amount to the TSP each pay period. It can be advantageous to contribute a percentage of pay because when you receive an increase in pay, your TSP contributions also automatically increase. You can stop, start, or resume TSP contributions at any time.

Should I save in the TSP?

The answer is a resounding: **YES**. The TSP should be a key element of *every* government employee's retirement plan.

FERS employees

For FERS participants, the TSP is intended to work in tandem with your government annuity and Social Security benefits. When it is time to retire, the savings in your TSP account will provide an additional source of income to supplement your annuity and Social Security benefits. When combined, your annuity, Social Security benefits, and TSP savings should provide an income similar to that of a CSRS participant. The amount of your contributions and your investment choices will help determine the date you retire and the lifestyle you'll have during retirement. If you don't save in the TSP, your income during retirement may not be adequate to meet your needs, and you certainly won't retire rich.

As a FERS employee, you're immediately eligible to receive two different types of contributions to your TSP account from your agency. Since there is no longer a waiting period, your agency will automatically contribute 1% of your basic pay to your TSP account each pay period. You'll receive these contributions even if you don't contribute any of your own money to your TSP account. If you contribute to your TSP account—and you need to contribute if you want to reach your retirement goal—then you'll also receive agency matching contributions on the first 5% of pay you contribute during each pay period. For example, if you contribute 5% of your basic pay to your TSP account, your agency will also contribute 5% to your account. Agency automatic contributions and agency matching contributions *do not* increase your pay for purposes of income tax or Social Security.

CSRS employees

Some CSRS participants choose not to save in the TSP because they don't receive matching contributions. This is a bit like refusing to eat dinner because you didn't get as much gravy as you wanted. Later on, you'll find that you're hungry and there still isn't any gravy. Unfortunately, if you wait too long, there won't be any dinner either. It's important to start participating in the TSP at a

relatively young age so you'll have time to enjoy the benefits of compounding. For CSRS participants, the TSP can supplement your annuity, helping you retire with more than enough income.

The benefits of saving in the TSP

In addition to providing you with a means of boosting your savings for retirement, the TSP offers other benefits. By contributing you can:

- **Lower your current taxable income.** When you save money in the TSP, you have an opportunity to reduce your taxable income. TSP contributions are made with pre-tax dollars. This means your current taxable income will be lower, and you may pay less in taxes today.

Basic monthly pay	TSP monthly contribution	Taxable income
$3,000	$0	$3,000
$3,000	$300	$2,700

- **Enjoy tax-deferred growth.** Your contributions to the TSP, and any earnings, grow tax-deferred. In other words, you don't pay taxes on any earnings until you withdraw money from your TSP account, and generally that's after you retire. As a result, you have an opportunity to earn interest on a larger amount of money over time which will give compound interest a chance to help your savings grow even faster.

- **Catch-up on saving for retirement.** If you are age 50 or older, and contribute the maximum to the TSP, you may be eligible to make additional catch-up contributions. Catch-up contributions are of particular benefit to participants who started saving for retirement later in life and want to make up for lost time. Before you can make catch-up contributions, you must meet the criteria for eligibility: 1) You must be age 50 or older by the end of the contribution year, and 2) You must already contribute the maximum amount to the TSP.

- **Access to your savings while you're employed.** If you need money for a financial emergency or a major purchase, you can take an in-service withdrawal from your TSP account. In-service withdrawals include hardship withdrawals and loans. Either option allows you to access the savings in your TSP account before retirement, but there are drawbacks.

  Hardship withdrawals: If you experience negative cash flow, extraordinary medical expenses, or other financial hardship, you may qualify for a *hardship withdrawal*. The cost of making a hardship withdrawal is high. You will owe taxes on the amount withdrawn and, if you are not yet age 59½, you will owe the IRS penalty of 10% of the amount withdrawn. In addition, when you make an in-service hardship withdrawal, you do not have an opportunity to repay the money you take from your account. Thus, you permanently deplete your retirement savings and forfeit any future earnings on the amount withdrawn.

  Loans: For some people, borrowing from their TSP account is the better option. When you take a loan, you repay the borrowed principal plus interest to your TSP account. You do not pay current taxes or the 10% early withdrawal penalty, so it can be a less costly option.

  There are still disadvantages to borrowing from your account. The interest you repay is unlikely to equal the amount your investments might have earned during the period you borrow. In addition, repaying the loan may be difficult. In some cases, participants are tempted to reduce their contributions, or to stop contributing to the TSP, which can hurt their long-term retirement saving goals.

  In addition, if you leave Federal service, you must repay your loan in full, including any interest on the outstanding principal. If you do not repay your loan, the TSP will declare a taxable distribution to you for your outstanding loan principal and interest. Ouch!

- **Take your savings with you when you leave employment.** Your contributions to the TSP (including any gains or losses) and agency matching contributions (including any gains or losses) are yours to take with you when you retire or leave government employment.

  Agency automatic (1%) contributions become yours gradually, over time, through a process called vesting. Vesting is an odd term, but it's

important to understand what it means. When you become "vested" in your TSP account, it means you have met all the service requirements necessary for you to keep the agency automatic 1% contributions made to your account. Most civilian employees become fully vested after three years of service—meaning they can take 100% of their agency automatic 1% contributions with them when they leave government employment. If you leave federal service before meeting vesting requirements, your agency automatic 1% contributions, and any earnings, will be forfeited to the TSP.

How do I invest my savings in the TSP?

For some people, the TSP is a wonderful opportunity because they get to decide how to invest the savings in their plan. For others, investing is a daunting task. Whether you are an experienced investor who enjoys building a portfolio or an inexperienced investor who does not enjoy the responsibility of investment decisions, the TSP has options that will meet your needs. Before you consider specific investments though, it's important to understand some basic principles of investing, including risk, reward, and diversification.

Understand risk

Risk means different things to different people. When you think about retirement and risk, what comes to mind? Some people worry about their health or the health of their spouses. Some worry about what they'll do once they stop working. Many people worry they'll outlive their savings. The point is that there are many different types of risks we face.

When it comes to investing, there are also different types of risk. As an investor, some of the most common investment risks you'll face include company risk, market risk, inflation risk, credit risk, and liquidity risk.

- **Company risk** is the chance you could lose some or all of your savings because a single company performs poorly. For example, your brother has a great idea and wants to start his own company. You choose to invest $5,000. If his company does well, he'll return your $5,000 plus a percentage of the profits. If the company does poorly, you could lose your entire investment.

The same risk is present when you invest in a company traded on an exchange. If you invest in the stock or buy the bonds of a single company, the performance of your investment is tied to the performance of that company. **A sound way to minimize company risk is to diversify by investing in the stocks and bonds of different companies.** That way, if one company does poorly, it has less of an impact on your savings. The TSP investments funds are all diversified portfolios so they offer some protection against company risk.

- **Market risk** is the chance you could lose some or all of your money as the result of a steep market decline. As you can see in the chart, markets move erratically from day to day or month to month, but over longer periods, trends emerge. Historically, over long periods, the market trend has been up.

S&P 500

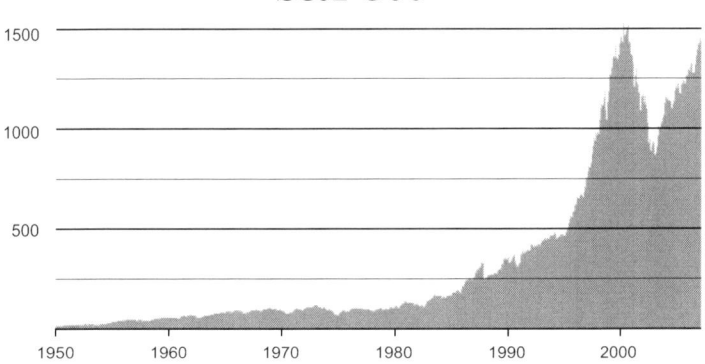

Different investments expose investors to different levels of market risk. Over the long-term, stocks are the investment with the greatest fluctuation. However, stocks have also historically provided the highest returns. When you invest in stocks, you have the greatest potential return and also the greatest exposure to market risk. Bonds offer lower potential returns than stocks and less exposure to market risk. Cash investments, such as Treasury Bills, offer the lowest potential returns and the least market risk. **A sound way to minimize market risk is to diversify by investing in stocks, bonds, and cash investments.**

- **Inflation risk** is the chance that the value of your savings will not keep pace with inflation over time. In order to minimize their exposure to market risk, some people will choose to invest all of their savings in cash

investment options because they perceive this to be a risk-free alternative. It is not. You read about the effect of inflation in the last chapter. Because the cost of goods and services we buy every day increases due to inflation, we need more money each year to keep pace with inflation. **A sound way to minimize inflation risk is to invest a portion of your savings in an investment that has historically outpaced inflation.** Generally, this means investing a portion of your savings in stocks.

• **Credit risk** is the possibility that a debt obligation—such as a bond—will default and fail to make either interest or principal payments, or both. When you purchase a bond, you are agreeing to lend a company a set amount of money. In return, the company agrees to pay you a set amount of interest over a certain period of time. At the end of that time, the company is expected to repay your loan. If the company fails to make its interest payments or to return your principal, it is in default.

You can limit credit risk by investing in bonds rated BBB or better by Standard & Poor's or Baa or better by Moody's. These are considered investment grade bonds. It's also a good idea to *diversify* your fixed income holdings by investing in bonds of several companies.

Bond ratings	S&P ratings	Moody's ratings
Investment grade bonds		
Highest quality	AAA	Aaa
High quality	AA	
Upper medium grade	A	A-1, A
Lower medium grade	BBB	Baa-1, Baa
Not investment grade bonds		
Speculative	BB	Ba
Highly speculative	B, CCC, CC	B, Caa, Ca
In default	D	C

• **Liquidity risk** is the possibility you will need your savings and be unable to access them immediately without accepting a loss. This is a risk that may have particular importance to investors who are

nearing or in retirement because they may need to liquidate some of their holdings each year to provide themselves with income.

- **Reinvestment risk** is the possibility that assets from maturing fixed-income investments cannot be reinvested at the same rate as before. For example, if you own a bond paying 7% interest that matures and current bonds available for investment are only paying 5% interest, this is reinvestment risk. This risk increases when interest rates begin to decline.

- **Political risk** is the chance of loss due to a change in governmental structure. Revolution and anarchy are ways of life in some less-developed countries having enormous growth potential, which can, of course, drastically affect the investment returns for those who take chances investing in these regions.

Diversification can help limit, although not eliminate, all the above risks. Keeping some of your savings in short-term, highly liquid investments like Treasury Bills or money market mutual funds can be a good idea to help limit liquidity and reinvestment risk.

The value of diversification

After reading about the various types of risk you may be exposed to when investing, I'm sure the importance of diversification is evident. Diversification can help investors limit the risks they face by spreading risk across different types of investments. If one investment or type of investment performs poorly, the chances are that its performance will be balanced by the stronger performance of another investment or type of investment.

The way you divide your savings among various types of investments should reflect your risk tolerance, time horizon, and other savings. If you are comfortable with the ups and downs of investing, or you have a long time before you retire, you may choose to invest your savings more aggressively. If you are not comfortable with investing, or you are nearing retirement, you may want to invest your savings more conservatively.

Before you select your strategy, you'll want to estimate the rates of return various strategies may provide over time and figure out which strategies offer returns that will help you reach your retirement goals. For example, if you need to earn 8% on average each year before retirement to reach your savings goal,

then investing 100% in Treasury bills and bonds is not a sound strategy. You'll need to invest a portion of your savings in stocks to boost your returns. If you're not comfortable investing more in stocks, you have other options. You can save more now, work longer, or reduce your lifestyle during retirement.

TSP investment choices

As a participant in the TSP, you can invest your account in any of the TSP investment funds, which include three stock funds, two fixed income funds, and five lifestyle funds:

- **Government Securities Investment (G) Fund**
- **Fixed Income Index Investment (F) Fund**
- **Common Stock Index Investment (C) Fund**
- **Small Capitalization Stock Index Investment (S) Fund**
- **International Stock Index Investment (I) Fund**
- **Lifecycle (L) Funds**

You can choose to invest your contributions to the TSP and any savings you've accumulated in any or all of the investment options available. It may be a good idea to invest in a diversified portfolio that includes stocks, bonds, and cash investments.

	Type of fund	Investment objective	Exposure to risk
G Fund	Government securities (specially issued to the TSP)	To provide long-term Treasury rates without risk of loss	• Inflation risk
F Fund	Bonds	To match the performance of the Barclays Capital U.S. Aggregate Index	• Credit risk • Market risk • Inflation risk
C Fund	Mid-sized and large company stocks	To match the performance of the S&P 500 Index	• Market risk • Inflation risk
S Fund	Small and mid-sized company stocks	To match the performance of the Dow Jones U.S. Completion Total Stock Market Index	• Market risk • Inflation risk
I Fund	International stocks	To match the performance of the Morgan Stanley Capital International EAFE Index	• Market risk • Inflation risk • Currency risk
L Funds	Includes G, F, C, S and I funds	To provide professionally diversified portfolios based on various time horizons	Risk based proportionally on risk in underlying funds

If you find the idea of making investment decisions daunting, you may want to invest in a lifecycle fund. Lifecycle funds gradually become more conservative as their target date nears. Of course, you should also consider enlisting the help of a knowledgeable and experienced investment professional who can help you select a portfolio that suits your needs.

Taking distributions from your account

When you leave government service to retire or move to the civilian sector, it's important to make informed decisions about the savings in your TSP account. In general, you have five options:

1. **Leave the money in your account**. You can elect to keep your savings in the TSP. If you choose this option, your savings can be left in the TSP until April 1 of the year following the year in which you reach age 70½, which is when the IRS requires you to begin taking minimum required distributions. At that time, you can choose to make a lump sum withdrawal or take monthly payments from the TSP or a TSP annuity vendor. If a withdrawal choice has not been made by this deadline, the Thrift Savings Board is required by law to purchase an annuity for you.

2. **Withdraw your entire account balance.** This is also called a single payment option. If your account balance is $3,500 or less, your account balance will automatically be paid to you in a single lump sum. If you have not yet reached age 59½, you may owe an early withdrawal penalty on your withdrawal.

   When you choose the single payment option, 20% of the value of your account will be withheld to cover federal income taxes applicable to the withdrawal. For example, if you have an account balance of $100,000 and request a single payment option, then $20,000 will be withheld for taxes and $80,000 will be sent to you.

   The IRS allows 60 days for you to roll over the full amount of your distribution to an IRA. If you roll over the full amount, including the amount you withheld for taxes, (you will need to find additional money to make up for the withheld amount) then you can avoid paying taxes on the amount of your withdrawal.

3. **Roll over your account balance.** If you dislike the idea of paying taxes on the entire balance of your TSP account, consider rolling over your account balance into another *tax-deferred* investment, like a traditional IRA, or a new employer's defined contribution retirement plan. When you roll over your savings, the money is sent directly to your IRA or plan provider and not to you, so taxes do not need to be withheld. There are many advantages to rollovers:

   • Your account balance continues to grow tax-deferred.

   • You have additional investment options.

   • You control access to your savings.

   • You avoid taxes and a penalty for early withdrawal if you're not age 59½.

   • You can also roll over your TSP account balance into a Roth IRA if you meet IRS income guidelines. However, you will have to pay taxes on the amount rolled over.

4. **Receive a series of monthly payments.** You can choose to withdraw the value of your account in a series of equal monthly payments. You select the number of payments you want to receive and the amount of each payment (must be at least $25). The payments will be made until your entire account balance has been distributed. Alternatively, you can choose to take payments for life. If you choose this option, your payments will be calculated based on your life expectancy. You cannot change the number or amount of these payments once they have begun; however, you can elect to receive a final single payment.

   If the series of payments is expected to last less than 10 years and is not calculated based on the IRS life expectancy table, the participant can have the TSP transfer all or part of each monthly payment to an IRA or another eligible retirement plan.

5. **Purchase an annuity**. If your account balance is greater than $3,500, you can use the funds in your TSP to purchase an annuity. Annuities are administered by insurance companies holding contracts with the Thrift Savings Board. You can purchase several different types of annuities and should become familiar with the options of each before you decide which is right for you. Your options include:

Single life annuity—An annuity paid only to you during your lifetime.

Joint life annuity with spouse—An annuity paid to you while you and your spouse are alive. When either of you dies, an annuity will be paid to the survivor for the rest of his or her life.

Joint life annuity with other survivor—An annuity paid to you while you and a person chosen by you (other than a spouse) are alive. This person must have an insurable interest in you. When either of you dies, an annuity will be paid to the survivor for life.

If you would like more detailed information about the TSP, visit the TSP web site at *www.tsp.gov*, or call the Thriftline at **1-TSP-YOU-FRST** (1-877-968-3778) or **1-TSP-THRIFT5** (1-877-847-4385) for hearing-impaired participants. You can also learn a great deal by reading the booklet *Withdrawing Your TSP Account After Leaving Federal Service*. It is available on the TSP website, from your agency, or from the TSP.

Chapter Review

1. Who can contribute to the TSP?

    a. CSRS employees
    b. FERS employees
    c. Both FERS and CSRS employees

2. Name three of the risks investors face.

3. Why is diversification a good investment strategy?

4. If you are not comfortable making investment decisions, what are two options available to you?

5. Which distribution options seem most attractive to you? Why?

Big Mistake #5

Using the wrong investment methodology

Investment professionals use a measure called "real rate of return" to gauge the effectiveness of various investments. Real rate of return measures the growth of an investment after taxes and inflation have been taken into account. For example, if you invest in a diversified portfolio that returns 8% over time, you pay 32% in state and federal taxes, and inflation averages 3.5% each year, then your real rate of return is just 1.9%.

	8%	5%
Investment return		
Take away combined state and federal taxes of 32% (.08 x .32), (.05 x .32)	- 2.6%	- 1.6%
Subtract average rate of inflation (3.5%)	- 3.5%	- 3.5%
Real rate of return	1.9%	- .1%

Historically, as you can see in the chart, only stocks have provided long-term rates of returns high enough to consistently offer investors positive real rates of return. As life expectancies increase, you'll need to rely on your retirement savings and investments to provide for longer periods of time. That means you need to earn positive real rates of return.

Chapter 6
A Benefits Primer

What was the biggest risk you took last week? Did you let your children walk to the store and back by themselves? Race a mountain bike down a steep hillside? Speak up about a difficult subject at work or at home? Risk means something different to each of us, but strategies for managing risk are generally universal. You can choose to:

- Avoid taking a risk—Don't let your children walk to the store alone.

- Limit the negative effects of the risk—Wear a helmet and protective gear as you race down the mountainside.

- Accept the consequences of taking the risk—Understand you may make enemies by speaking up, but you may find allies, too.

- Shift the risk to another party—Purchase insurance.

Managing risk is important. It's a way to protect things important to you. If it's important to you to preserve your wealth throughout your retirement, the government offers risk management tools—including health and life insurance benefits—that can help mitigate certain risks. In this chapter, you'll learn about these tools and how to manage them to your utmost advantage. You need to start planning early to ensure you'll have the risk management strategies you need in place during retirement.

Health insurance benefits

Health care coverage is expensive. How expensive is it? If you earn minimum wage and work 40 hours per week, participating in a private sector employer's health insurance plan will require 80% of your income for the year—if your employer's health care premiums are average.[1] No matter how much you earn, health care premiums are expensive, and the cost is increasing faster than the rate of inflation each year.

Health care is even more expensive for private sector workers after they retire. Those who choose to retire before age 65—the age at which they become eligible for Medicare coverage—are vulnerable to being priced out of the health care system because their share of the cost of employer-sponsored health care coverage, when it is extended into retirement, is almost four times the amount paid by working employees. On average, private sector retirees (of all ages) pay about 56% of the cost of their health care premiums.[2]

Federal Employees Health Benefits program

You're glad to be working in the public sector, aren't you? Under the Federal Employees Health Benefits (FEHB) Program, the federal government pays up to 75% of the cost of your health benefits coverage—even after retirement. In addition, FEHB not only covers federal employees and their families, it also covers retirees and their families. When you die, your survivor annuitants can continue to receive coverage through their CSRS or FERS retirement or survivor benefits.

As with everything else, there are some basic requirements that must be met if you want your coverage to carry over into retirement. You must have participated in an FEHB program for at least five years prior to retirement, and you must opt for an immediate annuity after retirement.

Requirement #1: Participate for five years preceding retirement

As a federal employee you must have been enrolled in an FEHB plan during the five years of service prior to your retirement. If you changed plans during that time, don't worry. What's important is continuous coverage under FEHB, not the specific plan. Coverage as a family member under another person's FEHB counts toward the requirement as well.

If you haven't been employed by the federal government for five years, then you must have been enrolled in FEHB for all service since you were first eligible to join the plan. If you left government employment and re-turned—as long as you re-enroll in the program within 60 days of returning to service—your break in service will not be treated as an interruption in the requirement.

Members of the Uniformed Services Health Benefits program must enroll in FEHB within 60 days of losing coverage for that time to be included as part of continuous FEHB coverage.

Continuing coverage for family members. If you would like family members to have coverage after you die, you must be enrolled in the 'Self and Family' option. In addition, at least one of your family members must be entitled to a survivor's annuity under CSRS or FERS.

Once your children reach age 22, they are no longer eligible for coverage, but they can elect Temporary Continuation of Coverage (TCC). The enrollee is responsible for paying the full amount of the premium, which allows coverage to be maintained for up to 36 months.

Discontinuing coverage. While there are some instances in which a retiree an-nuitant or survivor annuitant can suspend FEHB coverage (notably when they join a Medicare-sponsored Coordinated Care Plan), if you choose to discon-tinue coverage, you permanently lose access to the program. So if you retire from federal service and join the private sector, you may want to consider asking your new employer to provide you with cash rather than health care coverage. The additional income can pay your FEHB premiums.

If your new employer is not amenable to this plan, you may choose to main-tain your coverage by enrolling in an inexpensive FEHB plan. It's important to preserve your FEHB coverage into retirement, if at all possible. The risk of depleting your savings by paying the costs of treatment for a serious illness out-of-pocket must be effectively managed if you want to retire rich and stay that way. Health insurance is essential.

If you have retired from government and you're tempted to choose a private sector employer's coverage over FEHB, remember that many private sector em-ployers are discontinuing health care coverage for retirees, and those providing it often ask retired participants to shoulder a significant portion of the cost.

Requirement #2: Retire with an immediate annuity

A second requirement for continuing health care coverage into retirement is that you retire with an immediate annuity. This means your annuity must begin to accrue no later than one month after your final separation date. If you're considering taking a deferred annuity then you will not be eligible for FEHB coverage during your retirement.[3] If you have a deferred annuity, you may be covered by FEHB as a family member under a spouse's enrollment.

FERS employees who choose immediate retirement upon separation from government service have the option of postponing their annuity to avoid the age reduction. If you choose this option, when you begin receiving your postponed annuity you may re-enroll in FEHB as long as you meet the service eligibility requirements.

If you choose voluntary retirement, voluntary early retirement, discontinued service retirement, special provision retirement, or disability retirement and choose to take an immediate annuity, you may be eligible to receive FEHB benefits after retirement.

If you would like more detailed information about the FEHB Program, you should review *Pamphlet 79–2, FEHB Information for Retirees and Survivor Annuitants*. It's available through the U.S. Office of Personnel Management Website at *www.opm.gov*.

Understanding the need for long-term care

Another significant risk facing retirees today is outliving their savings. Some people just don't save enough before they retire; others deplete their savings paying long-term health care expenses. Long-term care is required when someone in your family needs daily assistance with medical care, daily activities, or other needs. It is a risk most American families face—and one for which few families are prepared. If a family is unprepared for the cost of long-term care, the consequences can be serious and affect several generations, as most long-term care is provided by families according to the National Council on Aging.

Despite this fact, a survey by the AARP found a majority of people under age 45 aren't as knowledgeable about long-term care as they need to be.[4] The survey found:

- 92% of participants could not accurately estimate (within 20%) the monthly cost of nursing home care.

- 59% think Medicare will pay for an extended nursing home stay—but it doesn't.

- 52% believe Medicare covers assisted living costs—but it doesn't.

Our ignorance does not bode well for the future. In order to effectively manage risk, people must understand it. You should know that after age 65 there is more than a 70% chance you will need some form of long-term care for some period of time.[5] The need for long-term care is not limited to older Americans, however. Nearly 40% of the people who need long-term care are younger than age 65.[6]

How much does long-term care cost?

The average annual cost for in-home care or care in nursing homes and assisted living facilities was more than $70,000 during 2006.[7] That's more than many people can afford, even if they have significant savings. It may be the reason that, according to the Kaiser Commission on Medicaid and the Uninsured, Medicaid has been the single largest source of funding for long-term care in recent years. Of course, to be eligible for Medicaid, you must be poor or have become poor paying long-term health care expenses. If your goal is to retire rich, relying on Medicaid to cover your long-term care costs is not a sound plan.

How do I know if I need long-term care insurance?

From a financial planner's point of view, if your savings cannot generate a stream of income large enough to cover your potential long-term care costs, then you need to purchase long-term care insurance. Let's consider Max and his wife, Erma. They have a CSRS annuity and rely on the income from the annuity to sustain their standard of living. They have also saved $250,000 in the TSP. Do they need a long-term care policy?

Yes. As a rule of thumb, if your savings cannot generate an annual stream of income large enough to pay for long-term care, then you should purchase a long-term care policy. In this instance, Max or Erma—whoever does not need long-term care—will continue to need the income from the annuity to live comfortably. Consequently, the money to pay for long-term care will need

to come from another source, generally personal savings or a long-term care insurance policy.

If the $250,000 in their TSP account earns 4% each year on average, it will generate about $10,000 in income each year. That's not nearly enough to pay for long-term care. Max and Erma would need to have savings of $1.75 million to be able to generate enough income to cover long-term care expenses today, and those expenses are increasing every year.

Purchasing long-term care insurance

Federal employees, retirees, active members of the Uniformed Services, and qualified family members can purchase long-term care insurance through the Federal Long Term Care Insurance Program (FLTCIP). The program offers a flexible benefits package that covers a variety of services detailed on the FLTCIP web site at *www.ltcfeds.com*. One of the most significant advantages of FLTCIP is that you don't have to answer health questions during open enrollment. If you or your spouse has a pre-existing condition of some sort, this long-term care policy may be a very good option.

It is not always the least expensive option, though. As with many group insurance opportunities, the healthy subsidize the less healthy. There are no spousal discounts and no discounts for good health in the FLTCIP program. In other words, there are no preferred rates, which a healthy individual might otherwise be eligible for with an outside insurer. If you're healthy, you may want to do some comparison shopping of long-term care policies.

	Cost of private LTC insurance per individual (standard health)[8]		Cost of Federal LTC insurance per individual[9]	
	• 3 years of coverage • 90-day waiting period • 5% compound inflation option		• 3 years of coverage • 90-day waiting period • 5% compound inflation option	
Daily benefit	$100	$150	$100 (Comprehensive 100)	$150 (Comprehensive 150)
Cost at age 55	$1,102/year	$1,653/year	$1,220/year	$1,831/year
Cost at age 65	$2,353/year	$3,530/year	$1,902/year	$2,853/year

At the end of the day, if you're not sure whether you need long-term care insurance, a CERTIFIED FINANCIAL PLANNER™ practitioner should be able to provide you with a financial household analysis to help determine the best way of handling your long-term care needs. Whatever you do, do not procrastinate about long-term care coverage—financial devastation is far more frightening than a few insurance premiums.

Managing risk with life insurance

Life insurance is another essential risk management tool. When you're young, the money from a life insurance policy can be used to generate income for your loved ones. It may ensure your children go to college or allow your spouse to keep your home. As you get older, life insurance can become an important estate planning tool.

The Federal Employees' Group Life Insurance (FEGLI) program offers an opportunity to purchase life insurance. FEGLI provides group term life insurance, which means it offers no cash value and no loan privileges. You are automatically enrolled in Basic FEGLI when you are first employed. You can enroll in additional programs during open enrollment periods; however, these occur quite infrequently. If you or your spouse is ill, you should watch for an open enrollment period, because you can purchase additional life insurance without answering any health questions.

The FEGLI program offers a variety of insurance options, including:

- **Basic FEGLI.** This coverage is equal to your salary, rounded up to the next $1,000, plus $2,000. For example, if you earn $33,400, Basic FEGLI will provide $36,000 of life insurance ($33,400 + $2,000 = $35,400. When you round up, you get $36,000.). Your agency pays one-third of the cost for this coverage.

- **Option A.** You can purchase $10,000 of additional coverage.

- **Option B.** You can purchase multiples of your salary (rounded up to the next $1,000), up to a maximum of five times your salary.

- **Option C.** You can purchase $5,000 to $25,000 of coverage for your spouse and $2,500 to $12,500 of coverage for each of your dependent children.

How much insurance do I need?

The only way to know how much insurance you should purchase is to evaluate how much money your family will need if you die. Most people will need about three to ten times their annual salary in life insurance. If you're retired, your children live outside the home, and you and your spouse have an annuity and savings to live on, then you may need very little coverage. If you have a young family and few savings, then you may need seven to ten times your annual salary in life insurance. If you're not sure how much you need, it's worth spending time with a planning professional who can evaluate your needs and make sure you have proper coverage.

Life insurance benefits during retirement

Life insurance benefits are available to you during retirement—as long as you meet some basic requirements. First, you must retire from federal service, not resign. Second, you must have been insured for the five years immediately preceding your retirement. If you haven't been employed for five years, then you must have participated since your first opportunity to enroll. Finally, you must not have converted your life insurance coverage to an individual policy. If you have already converted your policy, you may cancel the conversion to qualify for insurance benefits after retirement.

Because open enrollment occurs so rarely, it's important to think ahead when planning the amount of insurance you will need during retirement. Consider Xin's situation. He purchased $25,000 worth of coverage for his wife during the 2004 open enrollment. He also purchased three multiples of Option B coverage. If Xin retires in 2008, he will not be able to carry this additional coverage into retirement because he will not meet the requirement of having been insured during the five years prior to retirement. However, he will be able to retain any life insurance he had prior to 2003 during his retirement.

Paying your premiums

After retirement, you get to decide how much insurance you want to keep. The option you choose will influence the amount of your premiums. There are three basic choices:

1. **Basic coverage, 75% reduction**

   This option allows you to keep the Basic FEGLI coverage you enjoyed before retirement. When you reach age 65, or when you retire, whichever is later, you no longer have to pay premiums. Your coverage will be reduced by 2% each month until it levels off at 25% of the value of your original basic coverage.

2. **Basic coverage, 50% reduction**

   You continue paying a smaller premium after age 65, or when you retire, whichever is later, and your coverage is reduced by 1% each month until it levels off at 50% of the original value. You have the option to cancel this coverage reduction at any time and revert to the 75% reduction option.

3. **Basic coverage, no reduction**

   If you want to maintain the coverage you had on your last day of employment, you can choose to pay a premium from age 65, or from your retirement going forward, whichever is later. You have the option to cancel this coverage at any time and revert to the 75% reduction option.

You will also need to make a decision about some of the optional coverage you may want to keep during retirement.

- **Option A coverage**

  After you reach age 65, premium payments end, and your coverage will decline by 2% each month until it reaches 25% of its face value.

- **Option B or C coverage**

  If you have Option B or Option C coverage, you can choose full reduction or no reduction. With full reduction, your premium payments end and coverage will decline by 2% each month for 50 months. After 50 months, coverage ends. If you choose no reduction, you continue to pay premiums.

How does life insurance help you retire rich?

Throughout your life, life insurance helps protect you and your family against the risk of financial loss. When you're young, it protects your family. As you get older, it primarily protects your spouse. During retirement, it can help with estate planning.

Consider the example of Roberta, a 55-year-old, regular FERS employee. Her monthly annuity before reductions, with no survivorship option, is $3,052. If she elects the maximum survivor benefit so her husband will receive an annual income of about $20,140 after she dies, instead of receiving $3,052, Roberta will receive about $2,747 each month during her lifetime. The cost of the survivorship option during the first year is about $3,360. Over 20 years the cost is about $67,200, and over 30 years the cost is more than $100,000. What do you get for the price you are paying?

- Lifetime income for your spouse

- Access to health care benefits, regardless of insurability

- Cost of living adjustments to help income keep pace with inflation— payable beginning at age 62

Is it worth it? It might be. It's also possible that you could use the 10% of lost income to purchase a life insurance policy to provide greater value to your spouse after your death. It's a good idea to consider your family's total financial resources before you make a decision.

Chapter Review

1. Why is risk management important?

2. Name two requirements you must meet to carry your FEHB benefits into retirement.

3. Name three requirements you must meet to carry your FEGLI benefits into retirement.

4. Imagine your spouse has Alzheimer's Disease. What will life be like if you have long-term care insurance? What will life be like if you don't?

5. What are the benefits of a survivorship annuity?

Notes

[1] Towers Perrin HR Services. "2007 Health Care Cost Survey." Web. 28 Oct. 2009. <http://www.towersperrin.com/tp/getwebcachedoc?webc=HRS/USA/2007/200703/07HCCSFinal.pdf>.

[2] Ibid.

[3] You qualify for a deferred annuity if you are covered by CSRS or FERS, have more than five years of civilian service, but resign before you meet the age and service requirements needed to receive immediate benefits.

[4] AARP. "The Costs of Long-Term Care: Public Perceptions Versus Reality in 2006." AARP, Dec. 2006. Web. 28 Oct. 2009. <http://assets.aarp.org/rgcenter/health/ltc_costs_2006.pdf>.

[5] American Society on Aging. *Americans Fail to Act on Long-Term Care Protection.* American Society on Aging, 23 May 2003. Web. 28 Oct. 2009. <http://www.asaging.org/media/pressrelease.cfm?id=35>.

[6] Thompson, Lee. "Long-Term Care: Support for Family Caregivers." Georgetown University, Long-Term Care Financing Project, Mar. 2004. Web. 28 Oct. 2009. <http://ltc.georgetown.edu/pdfs/caregivers.pdf>.

[7] Genworth Financial, USA. "Yearly Long Term Care Costs Move Above $70,000 in 2006." Medical News Today, 28 Mar. 2006. Web. 28 Oct. 2009. <http://www.medical-newstoday.com/articles/40403.php>.

[8] Estimated premium cost obtained from a private insurance brokerage service.

[9] *FLTCIP Premiums Calculation.* The Federal Long Term Care Insurance Program. Web. 28 Oct. 2009. <https://www.ltcfeds.com/ltcWeb/do/assessing_your_needs/ratecalcOut>.

Big Mistake #6

Choosing incorrect types and amounts of insurance

At the beginning of your career, your biggest asset is your future earnings. Therefore, life insurance is very important. If you die young, your heirs will never benefit from those earnings. That is the reason most young families need five to seven times their gross annual income in life insurance, and some may need even more than that. You should determine your life insurance needs based on your life circumstances. Your age, debt levels, dependent status, income, and net worth are all factors that should be considered.

In the natural cycle of events, the risk of dying too soon eventually will be replaced by the risk of living too long. As you get older and your family members become independent, your risk management priorities may change. A skilled financial planning professional can help you make sound risk management decisions throughout your life.

Chapter 7
Social Security and Medicare

Urban legends are a kind of modern folklore. While some may have a kernel of truth, generally they are exaggerated or distorted. Regardless, these stories are told and retold until they become a part of our culture. Although myths about Social Security and Medicare are not as exciting as tales of alligators in New York City's sewers, or the woman who was killed when spiders invaded her elaborate hairdo, they are prevalent. Some myths common among private sector workers include:

- Social Security will provide enough income to allow me to retire comfortably.

- I will be eligible to receive full Social Security benefits if I retire at age 65.

- Medicare will cover my medical, hospitalization, and long-term care costs after I retire.

For public sector workers, the myths are a bit different:

- I have a FERS annuity. In tandem with Social Security benefits, it will provide all the income I need for retirement.

- I have a CSRS annuity so Social Security won't affect me.

- I worked in the private sector and the public sector so I will receive my CSRS annuity and Social Security benefits.

- My spouse works in the public sector so I will get Social Security benefits through him or her even though I have a CSRS annuity.

The unhappy ending for many of these myths is that you overestimate your retirement income and have to reduce your standard of living when you retire.

Social Security and Medicare are complicated topics. It's not my intention to provide detailed descriptions of the programs in this chapter. What you will find is a broad overview of the benefits the programs provide. After reading the chapter you should understand the types of benefits you can expect to receive from these programs. Let's begin by considering Social Security retirement, disability, and spousal benefits, and then we'll take a look at Medicare.

The history of Social Security

During the 1930s, America faced one of the worst economic crises in its history. The Great Depression had created widespread unemployment. About two million men, often called hobos, wandered the country looking for work. Banks and businesses failed. People with jobs clung to them. By the middle of the decade, it's estimated that less than one-half of older Americans had enough income to be self-supporting.

It was clear people needed help. After taking office, President Roosevelt was deluged with letters asking for help. See the sample letter on the following page. Public desperation was the driving force behind the creation of a social insurance system. Many people had strong opinions. However, it was just as difficult for Americans to decide what kind of system to implement back then as it is for us to decide how to fix the system today.

The system eventually signed into law a pay-as-you-go social insurance program intended to provide economic security to the citizens of our country. Most American workers pay Federal Insurance Contribution Act (FICA) payroll taxes to help fund Social Security and Medicare. These taxes are not set aside to pay future benefits. Instead, they are used to pay benefits to current Social Security and Medicare recipients. The system was restructured several times during the 1900s, most recently during the early 1980s, when a committee headed by Alan Greenspan made adjustments that cut benefits and increased revenues for the program.

July 3, 1933

Dear Sir,

I write to ask you about securing an old age pension for my mother…She is helpless and suffering from Sugar Diabetes, which has affected her mind. She has to be cared for in the same manner as an infant. She is out of funds completely. Her son whom she used to keep house for is in a hospital in Waco, Texas—no compensation for either himself or her.

I am a widow; have spent all my savings caring for her. I have kept boarders and roomers in a private home to keep my four children for I have always been a lady; this is why I appeal to you to place your dear mother in my dear mother's place—with no money and no place to go unless it be to the poor house, I cannot rent my rooms now for she demands constant care and attention. Please do something about this request as soon as possible.

She will be 82 years old on August 9th...

PS: I do not own my home and at present I cannot meet my bills (overdue). I don't know what to expect next. Thank you in advance.

Social Security eligibility

Depending on the type of annuity you intend to receive from the government, you may or may not be eligible for Social Security benefits. FERS annuitants are eligible for Social Security. As you may recall from earlier chapters, FERS is a tandem program intended to provide pension income to supplement Social Security retirement benefits. CSRS annuitants may, in some circumstances, qualify to receive Social Security benefits through a spouse who worked in the private sector. The rules guiding eligibility if you have a CSRS retirement annuity are often complex. We'll look more closely at the government offset provision and windfall elimination provision affecting CSRS employees later in this chapter.

FERS participants and Social Security

To qualify for Social Security, you must work and pay the FICA tax. In addition, you need to accumulate 40 credits. One quarter of credit is equal to $1,090 in FICA covered wages in 2009, and you can earn up to four credits each year, as determined by your earnings. As a result, most people need 10 years of work to qualify for Social Security retirement benefits. Disability benefits and survivor's benefits often require fewer credits.

If you earn enough credits, the Social Security benefit you receive will be a percentage of your lifetime income. It's important to remember that although we all pay the same percentage of FICA tax, we do not all receive the same Social Security retirement benefits. Lower-income workers receive a higher percentage of their average lifetime earnings than people with higher earnings. If you have average earnings, you can expect a retirement benefit to replace about 40% of your average lifetime income. If you earned more than an average income, you can expect Social Security to replace a smaller percentage of your pre-retirement income.

The Social Security portion of the FICA tax pays for three types of social insurance: retirement insurance, disability insurance, and survivor's insurance.

Retirement insurance

Do you know the age at which you can retire and receive full Social Security benefits? If you said 65, you're only right if you were born before 1938. Contrary to common belief, age 65 is not the standard retirement age. As you

can see in the following table, people born after 1938 are not eligible for full benefits until they've passed age 65.

Year of Birth	Full Retirement Age
Before 1938	65
1938	65 and 2 months
1939	65 and 4 months
1940	65 and 6 months
1941	65 and 8 months
942	65 and 10 months
1943-1954	66
1955	66 and 2 months
1956	66 and 4 months
1957	66 and 6 months
1958	66 and 8 months
1959	66 and 10 months
1960 and After	67

Of course, you don't have to retire at your full retirement age. You can choose to apply for early Social Security retirement benefits as early as age 62. If you do, your benefits will be reduced by a fraction of a percent for each month that you retire before your full retirement age. You may also choose to delay retirement. If you choose to retire later than your full retirement age, you are eligible to receive a higher benefit.

No matter when you choose to apply for Social Security retirement benefits, you don't have to stop working. You can apply for early, full, or delayed retirement benefits and continue to work. Working after retirement can be a double-edged sword. The bad news is that your benefits may be reduced if you retire prior to your full retirement age and you earn more than a certain amount of income. The good news is that your additional income may increase the benefits you are eligible to receive later in retirement.

Disability insurance

The immortality of youth is an illusion, as many of us learn later in life. When it comes to disability, there is a 3 in 10 chance that a 20-year-old worker will become disabled before reaching retirement age, according to the Social Security Administration. To protect people who become unable to work, and their families, Social Security pays disability insurance benefits through two programs: the Social Security disability insurance program and the Supplemental Security Income (SSI) program.

The definition of disability that Social Security uses is quite strict, however. To qualify for benefits, you must:

- Be severely physically or mentally impaired so that the impairment prevents any substantial gainful activity.

- Have a disability that is expected to last at least 12 months, or result in death.

- Have the required number of quarters (or credits) of coverage at the time you are disabled.

It is often easier to qualify as disabled under FERS or CSRS than under Social Security. CSRS employees do not qualify to receive Social Security disability benefits. However, if you are receiving disability benefits through FERS, and you qualify for Social Security disability benefits, your FERS benefits may be reduced as a result. You can learn more by reading the FERS pamphlet RI 98-2, *Information for Disability Annuitants.*

Survivors insurance

If you have earned enough credits, Social Security can provide partial income replacement for your family when you die. The number of credits needed depends on your age at death. The younger you are, the fewer credits you need. If you are eligible, Social Security will pay survivor benefits to your widow or widower (even if you are divorced), children, or dependent parents. Benefits can be paid to your children, and a spouse who is caring for them, if you have accumulated credit for one and one-half years of work (six credits) during the three years before your death.

Social Security benefits

If you would like to learn more about Social Security benefits, or get a quick estimate of your benefits, visit the Social Security website at *www.ssa.gov.* Also, keep an eye on the mail. Each year, about one month before your birthday, Social Security sends a benefits statement documenting your earned income and estimated benefits. Make sure you review it for accuracy. If there are errors within the past three years, they can be corrected fairly easily. If the errors are further in the past, the correction process becomes more complicated.

CSRS and Social Security benefits

If you are covered by a CSRS annuity, you do not pay Social Security taxes, although you do pay the portion of FICA going toward Medicare. If you believe you will never have to think about Social Security because you have a CSRS annuity, think again. Many CSRS employees have also worked in the private sector, or they have a small business. As a result, they may have paid FICA on a considerable amount of earnings, and are eligible to receive benefits from Social Security. If you fall into this category, it is important to know about the Windfall Elimination Provision (WEP).

As a CSRS annuitant, you may be married to someone who has worked in the private sector. If your spouse has been paying FICA taxes and earning Social Security credits, then you may be eligible to receive Social Security survivor's benefits one day. If so, you must understand the Government Pension Offset (GPO).

The Windfall Elimination Provision

The Windfall Elimination Provision (WEP) will reduce the amount of your Social Security benefits if you receive a pension based on work for an employer that did not withhold Social Security taxes from your salary, such as a government agency or an employer in another country. Of course, there are exceptions. WEP does not apply if:

- You were first hired by the government after December 31, 1983.

- You were employed on December 31, 1983, by a nonprofit organization that initially did not withhold Social Security taxes, but
  subsequently began to withhold them.

- You have paid Social Security taxes on all work performed
  since 1957.

- You have accumulated 30 or more years of substantial earnings
  under Social Security.

Social Security benefits are based on your average monthly earnings, adjusted for inflation. If you are subject to WEP, the formula used to calculate your benefit amount is modified, giving you a lower benefit than your annual Social Security benefit estimate statements have shown. If you would like to know how your Social Security Benefits may be affected by WEP, visit the Social Security website at *www.ssa.gov*. They have a WEP calculator, which can provide a detailed estimate.

The Government Pension Offset

When Social Security was established in the early 1900s, many women did not work. To protect them and ensure they had adequate income, Social Security allocated up to 50% of a worker's Social Security benefit to one's dependent wife. If a worker died, his widow could get as much as 100% of his benefit. During the 1970s, the Supreme Court ruled that men could receive spousal benefits as well.

About the same time, the Government Pension Offset (GPO) was created. GPO paved the way for individuals who received pensions from federal, state, or local governments based on work that did not require them to pay Social Security taxes, to have their spousal, widow's, or widower's benefits reduced. The reduction is significant—up to two-thirds of the monthly pension amount received, which can actually eliminate the spousal, widow's, or widower's Social Security benefits. For example, if you receive a monthly civil service pension of $900, then two-thirds of that amount, or $600, will be deducted from your spousal, widow's, or widower's Social Security benefits. There are some exceptions to the GPO. If you would like to learn more, please read the Social Security Publication called *Government Pension Offset*. It can be found on the Social Security website at *www.ssa.gov*.

Example : The Government Pension Offset

Elizabeth receives a CSRS monthly benefit of $3,000. She is eligible to receive a spousal Social Security benefit of $800. To calculate her offset, she multiplies $3,000 by 2/3. The result is $2,000. Once she subtracts $2,000 from the benefit for which she is eligible—$800—her benefit is entirely eliminated.

$3,000 pension benefit
x 2/3

$2,000 offset amount

$800 Social Security benefit
- $2,000 offset amount

Less than zero

Elizabeth's Social Security benefit is completely eliminated by the GPO.

The history of Medicare

Medicare is the fourth part of our current Social Security program. It was initiated in 1965 by President Lyndon Johnson, and former President Truman received the very first Social Security card. The new social insurance program extended health coverage to most Americans who were age 65 or older. During its first three years of existence, nearly 20 million people enrolled in Medicare. Today, Medicare provides health insurance to people age 65 or older, and to people younger than age 65 who have certain types of disabilities.

If you want to retire rich and maintain your wealth throughout retirement, you need to estimate your post-retirement health costs, including Medicare premiums, deductibles, and co-payments. This means you must understand what Medicare does and does not offer, and plan to fill any gaps in your health care coverage. There are many ways to plan for your health care needs during retirement; however, effective strategies often include a combination of Medicare, personal health insurance, and personal savings.

Medicare programs and services

You are responsible for selecting the Medicare options best suited to your needs. Your costs will vary depending on your plan, coverage, and services. You can choose to participate in the original Medicare plan, or in Medicare Advantage

Plans like HMOs and PPOs. In addition, you'll need to decide which prescription drug plan is most favorable for you.

The original Medicare plan

If you have paid Medicare taxes while working and have earned enough credits to qualify for Social Security, you will receive **Medicare Part A** coverage without paying a monthly premium. Part A coverage helps pay for inpatient care in hospitals, including critical access hospitals and skilled nursing facilities. Part A does not cover the cost of custodial or long-term care. However, it does help cover home health care and hospice care if you qualify for these benefits.

You'll also have the option to enroll in **Medicare Part B**, which helps cover medical services, such as doctors' visits, outpatient care, and other medically necessary services not covered by Medicare Part A. Part B may also help pay for some preventive services, such as exams, lab tests, and screenings to help prevent, find, or manage medical problems. If you choose Part B coverage, you will pay a monthly premium to receive coverage, and you will have an annual deductible amount.

If you don't enroll in Part B when you are first eligible, the cost of this coverage will increase by 10% each full 12-month period you could have enrolled but chose not to enroll.

Medicare Advantage Plans

Medicare Advantage Plans are sometimes called Medicare Part C. They combine the coverage offered through Medicare Part A and Part B. Part C coverage is offered through private insurance companies approved by Medicare. Your costs will depend on the coverage you choose. You can participate in a Medicare:

- Health Maintenance Organization (HMO) Plan

- Preferred Provider Organization (PPO) Plan

- Private Fee-for-Service (PFFS) Plan

- Special Needs Plan

- Medical Savings Account (MSA) Plan

Most Medicare Advantage Plans offer Medicare prescription drug coverage. If you join an Advantage Plan and want drug coverage, you are required to get it from your plan.

Prescription drug coverage

Through Medicare Part D, Medicare offers prescription drug coverage to everyone enrolled in Medicare. Private firms approved by Medicare offer Part D coverage. Most drug plans charge a monthly premium. Your cost will depend on the plan you choose. The Part D premium must be paid over and above the premium you pay for Part B coverage.

Choosing your coverage

Medicare offers many options, and your costs can vary greatly depending on the choices you make. If you have the time and inclination to do your own research, you should read *Medicare and You*. The handbook provides detailed information about Medicare and can be found at *www.medicare.gov*. If you don't have the desire to complete this research on your own, I suggest you find a professional financial planner who can help you understand the alternatives available.

The cost of health care is one of the biggest threats to your ability to preserve wealth during retirement. Medicare will not be able to cover all of your health care needs after you retire. It does not offer any kind of long-term care coverage at all, and we discussed the need for long-term care thoroughly in the last chapter. If you want to retire rich, you need to understand and plan for your health care needs.

Chapter Review

1. What type of annuity is likely to cause its recipient's Social Security benefits to be reduced?

    a. CSRS
    b. FERS
    c. CSRS Offset
    d. All of the above
    e. Only a and c

2. What is WEP? How is it different from GPO?

3. What is your full retirement age under Social Security?

4. Under what conditions will you apply for Social Security early retirement benefits?

5. Under what conditions will you apply for delayed Social Security retirement benefits?

Big Mistake #7

Not having a plan to address long-term care expenses

It is the classic good news, bad news scenario. The good news is: We're living longer than ever before. The bad news is: More people than ever before are at risk of outliving their savings. The cost of long-term care can wipe out sizeable savings in less than a decade.

If you're lucky enough to be retiring with a substantial nest egg you've worked hard to save, it's important to manage the risk that you or your spouse may need long-term care. You need to make a plan and decide how to cover the costs. Will you be able to save enough so that you can pay for long-term care out-of-pocket? Or will you need to purchase a long-term care insurance policy? While you are at it, you should talk with your parents about whether they have plans in place to cover their need for long-term care.

The Titanic was unsinkable—until it hit an iceberg! Envision yourself as the Titanic. You've worked hard to attain financial security, and you want to preserve it. Long-term care is the iceberg in your path. It's a mistake not to plan a course of action that will allow you to stay afloat.

"The taxpayer — that's someone who works for the federal government but doesn't have to take the civil service examination."
~ Ronald Reagan

"Taxes are what we pay for civilized society."
~ Oliver Wendell Holmes, Jr., U.S. Supreme Court Justice

"The hardest thing in the world to understand is the income tax."
~ Albert Einstein

Chapter 8
Income Tax Considerations

Everyone has an opinion about income taxes. Whether you hate them or think they're essential in a civilized society, you need to control the amount you pay in taxes if you want to preserve the wealth you've accumulated during your working years. Unfortunately, the tax code is complex, and it changes frequently. Before you make decisions about how to manage your retirement savings, it may be best to enlist the assistance of a certified public accountant or financial planning professional who can provide expertise in tax matters before taking action. If you make a mistake, the consequences can be costly.

In the following pages you'll learn about the ways in which current taxes affect your pension, TSP, and Social Security benefits. Before we delve into the specifics of taxation, let's discuss the common myth: You'll be in a lower tax bracket after you retire.

Will you really be in a lower tax bracket after you retire?

It's not very likely. Decades ago, when there were many, many tax brackets, it was normal for individuals who retired to drop into a lower tax bracket because they received less income. Today, there are just a few tax brackets, and each one covers a broad range of income. Unless you are very close to the baseline income for a tax bracket, it's unlikely that your earnings will fall significantly enough after you retire for you to change brackets.

Understanding your marginal tax rate

It may surprise you to learn that if you're in the 35% tax bracket, you don't really pay 35% of your income in taxes. The U.S. income tax is a graduated tax, which means you pay a different percentage of tax on different amounts of income. For example, as you can see in the table, during 2009, American taxpayers will owe: 10% on income up to $8,350; 15% on income from $8,350 up to $33,950; and so on.

2009 Tax Table

Tax rate	Single	Married (filing jointly)
10%	$0 to $8,350	0 to $16,700
15%	$8,350 up to $33,950	$16,700 to $67,900
25%	$33,950 up to $82,250	$67,900 to $137,050
28%	$82,250 up to $171,550	$137,050 to $208,850
33%	$171,550 up to $372,950	$208,850 to $372,950
35%	Above $372,950	Above $372,950

Consider Marvin and Ishtar who are in the 25% tax bracket. They are married and file taxes jointly. Their taxable income was $80,000 in 2009. Once the various tax rates are applied to different amounts of income, they owe $12,375 in taxes, or about 15% in taxes. After retirement, they plan to have 90% of their pre-retirement income, or $72,000. They'll still be in the 25% tax bracket. Will their taxes be lower? Yes—by $2,000 per year.

Rule of 8. In general, I use 8% as a rule of thumb for estimating marginal tax rates. I just subtract eight from my client's tax bracket, which gives me an estimate of their marginal tax rate. Like most rules of thumb, it's not perfectly accurate.

Taxation of civil service annuity benefits

Your civil service annuity benefits are taxed as ordinary income. However, when you begin receiving benefits from a civil service retirement annuity, only a portion of the amount you receive will be subject to taxation. That's because some of the money you receive is considered to be a tax-free return of the contributions you've made to the plan. Since you've already paid taxes on those contributions, you won't be taxed again when they are distributed to you. Any interest or dividends your annuity may have earned over the years will be taxed.

Different methods may be used to figure out how much of your annuity payments are attributable to your contributions and how much are attributed to investment earnings. The method you use will depend on your annuity starting date. The **Simplified Method** should be used if your annuity starting date is November 18, 1996, or later. Under the Simplified Method, you figure the taxable and tax-free parts of your annuity payments by completing the Simplified Method Worksheet in the IRS Form 1040 Instructions or IRS Form 1040A Instructions or in IRS Publication 575, *Pension and Annuity Income.*

Summary: Taxable Portion of an Annuity

- Cost is recovered tax-free

- Cost = your contributions

- Tax-free part = your cost ÷ a number of months based on your age

- Taxable portion of annuity is shown on Form CSA 1099R

- After cost is recovered, full amount of annuity is taxable

- If full amount of cost is not recovered at your (or the survivor annuitant's) death, a deduction is allowed for the unrecovered cost

  - Claimed on your (or survivor's) final tax return as a miscellaneous itemized deduction

Example: At annuity start date (1/1/09) John is age 65 and his wife, Jane, is age 57. John's monthly annuity is $1,000 at a cost of $31,000.

1. Total annuity payments:	$12,000
2. Total cost:	$31,000
3. Number from Table (see below):	310
4. Divide line 2 by 3:	$100
5. Multiply line 4 by number of months for which this year's payments were made:	$1,200
6. Enter any amounts previously recovered tax-free:	0
7. Subtract line 6 from line 2:	$31,000
8. Enter the smaller of line 5 or line 7:	$1,200
9. **Taxable amount for year:** Subtract line 8 from line 1. Enter result, but not less than zero.	$10,800

No Survivor Annuity

IF your age on your annuity starting date was	*THEN enter on line 3*
55 or under	360
56-60	310
61-65	260
66-70	210
71 or over	160

Survivor Annuity

IF the annuitants' combined ages on your annuity starting date were	*THEN enter on line 3*
110 or under	410
111-120	360
121-130	310
131-140	260
141 or over	210

If your annuity starting date is before November 19, 1996, you may choose either the Simplified Method or the General Rule Method. The **General Rule Method** requires that you calculate the taxable and tax-free parts of your annuity payment using IRS life expectancy tables. You can learn more by reading IRS Publication 939, *General Rules for Pensions and Annuities.*

Whether you use either of these methods, the tax-free portion of your benefit payments will be a set dollar amount that remains constant, even if your annuity increases in value over time. Generally, this rule applies for as long as you receive an annuity, which means all cost of living increases are taxable.

State taxes

If paying less in taxes after you retire is important, you may wish to relocate to a state offering federal retirees a tax break. Ten states exempt annuities from taxation, and seven states don't have any income taxes. Before you move, however, find out whether the state you're considering assesses other types of taxes. Often states without income taxes make up for the loss of revenue through higher sales, property, and other taxes. Make sure you figure out what your income will be—net of all taxes—before deciding where to move.

Refunds—No, it's not about getting money back

When you leave your position to retire or work outside the federal government and you are not eligible for an immediate annuity, you can choose to receive a deferred annuity at age 62, or ask for a refund of the savings in your CSRS or FERS retirement account. If you choose a refund, you lose future annuity rights unless you are re-employed by CSRS or FERS and work for a long enough period to again qualify for benefits. Your personal situation will determine whether it is more beneficial for you to leave savings in the fund or take a refund. Before you choose to take a refund, however, make sure you have read the Refunds chapter in the *CSRS/FERS Handbook* which can be found on the OPM website at *www.opm.gov.*

Taxes and your TSP investment savings account

The savings in your TSP account will be an important part of your wealth after retirement so it's important to make informed decisions about withdrawing the funds you've saved. First, you need to recognize that contributions you

make to the TSP while you are working are tax-deferred, as are any agency matching contributions and any earnings in your account. As a result, your account has an opportunity to grow and compound tax-deferred until you begin to make withdrawals.

As you approach retirement, you'll want to consider the options available to you. For some people, leaving savings in their retirement plan may be the best choice. The early retirement age for the TSP is age 55. (The early retirement age for IRAs and other qualified plans is 59½.) That means you can withdraw savings from your TSP account without an early withdrawal penalty beginning at age 55.

If you would prefer to move your savings, you can make a partial withdrawal or withdraw the full value of your TSP account through:

- A single payment

- A series of monthly payments

- A life annuity

- Some combination of these options

The option you choose can have a profound effect on the value of your retirement savings.

Option 1: A single payment

Beware of the single payment. This is the least attractive of the options in my opinion. When you take a single payment, whether it is a full or partial payment, you will owe ordinary income taxes on the payment amount. If you are not yet age 55, you will also owe a 10% penalty on the payment amount.

For example, imagine that a hypothetical plan participant, Michaela, age 53, has saved $425,000 in her TSP account and chooses a lump sum payment. The $425,000 distributed to her will be treated as ordinary income in the year she receives it. Not only will she not drop into a lower tax bracket—she'll shoot up into the top tax bracket.

Example: Michaela, age 53, has $425,000 in her TSP account.

	Single payment	Direct rollover to an IRA
Amount of withdrawal:	$425,000	$425,000
Income tax owed:	- $114,750	- $0
Penalty tax owed:	-$42,500	- $0
Total after-tax value:	**$267,750**	**$425,000**

Applying the "Rule of 8" to 2009 tax tables, Michaela's marginal tax rate will be about 27% (35% - 8%). She'll owe approximately $114,750 in taxes on her distribution. Since she is not yet age 55, she'll owe another 10%, or $42,500, in penalty taxes. (She'll pay her penalty tax when she files her tax return the following year.) This means she owes almost one-third of the value of her savings to the IRS for taxes! After all is said and done, she'll be left with only $267,750.

Pros and cons of single payments

Advantages	Disadvantages
• Immediate, unrestricted use of your savings.	• You owe current federal and state taxes unless assets are rolled over within 60 days.
• You may be eligible for favorable tax treatment.	• You may owe a 10% early withdrawal penalty on the amount of the payment.
	• Your withdrawal will be reduced by 20% mandatory withholding for income taxes.

Single payments and indirect rollovers

If you have already taken a single payment, you can roll over the money you've received to a traditional IRA or a new employer's plan within 60 days. If you rollover the full amount of the distribution within the allotted time, you can avoid paying taxes and penalties.

There's a catch, however. Before sending a single payment distribution, the Office of Personnel Management is required to withhold 20% for income taxes. This means you receive 80% of the value of your account. If you roll over 80% of your account, that amount can continue to grow tax-deferred. The 20% withheld, however, will be taxed. If your goal is to avoid paying current taxes altogether, you need to make up the withheld 20% out of your own pocket. For this reason, if you know you are going to roll over your savings, a direct rollover, discussed later in this chapter, may be your best choice.

You don't have to be an accountant to recognize that taking a single payment can greatly reduce the wealth you accumulate. As you plan for your retirement, it's essential to find ways to preserve your wealth, keep it invested, and (hopefully) growing so that you have more than enough money throughout your retirement. Taking a single payment is rarely going to help you accomplish these goals. Fortunately, there are better options available.

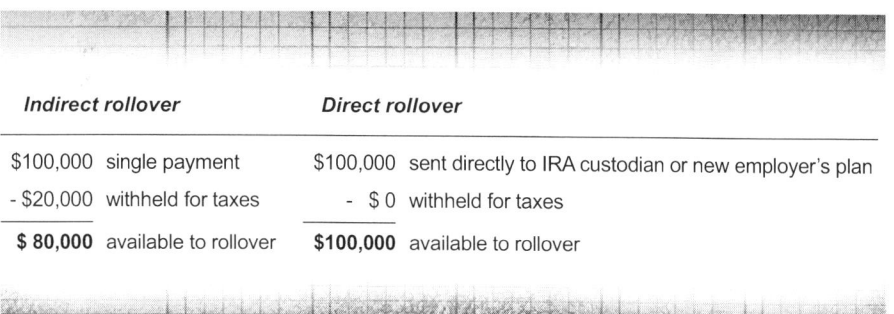

Indirect rollover		*Direct rollover*	
$100,000	single payment	$100,000	sent directly to IRA custodian or new employer's plan
- $20,000	withheld for taxes	- $ 0	withheld for taxes
$ 80,000	available to rollover	**$100,000**	available to rollover

Direct rollovers

If you would prefer to keep your savings invested and preserve the tax advantages you enjoy in the TSP, then a rollover may be a better option. You can roll over your savings into an IRA by asking the Office of Personnel Management

to transfer your savings to your IRA account. A direct rollover is a great way to shelter the wealth in your TSP account and keep it growing tax-deferred. The key is that your TSP savings must go directly from the TSP to your IRA custodian. This is called a trustee-to-trustee transfer, and it allows you to avoid taxes and penalties.

Pros and cons of direct rollovers

Advantages	Disadvantages
• You avoid current income taxes.	• The early retirement age is 59½ for IRAs rather than 55, as it is with the TSP.
• Your savings may continue to grow tax-deferred.	• Required minimum distributions must begin once you reach age 70½ .
• You may have more investment choices.	• No loans are allowed from IRAs
• You have flexibility.	
• You can pass your savings on to heirs tax-efficiently.	

An IRA gives you great flexibility. You can work with your financial planner to choose the IRA custodian that best meets your needs. IRA custodial agreements differ. If you want to have the ability to do different things—like stretching payments over the lifetimes of your beneficiaries—it's important to make sure the IRA you choose allows it. Once you've chosen an IRA custodian, opened an account, and transferred your savings into it, you can select investments for your account.

IRAs can provide estate planning advantages as well. One of the most important advantage is a spouse *or* non-spouse beneficiary can inherit your IRA and stretch the amount received over his or her life expectancy, which can help reduce taxes for the beneficiary. If you have more than one beneficiary, establishing an IRA for each heir allows each one to receive payments from the IRA (after it is inherited) based on his or her life expectancy. This is particularly important if your beneficiaries are different ages. If they all inherit one IRA, distributions must be paid over the life expectancy of the oldest beneficiary. Your financial planner can help you determine the strategy that best suits your needs.

The rules that apply to IRAs are slightly different than the rules for the TSP. First, withdrawals made before age 59½ are subject to penalty tax. Second, you must begin taking distributions from an IRA by age 70½.

The IRA is registered in your name so you retain complete control over the assets. This means you can make withdrawals when you need income. The amount of taxes you pay will be determined by the amount you withdraw during any given year, your age, and other sources of income.

Roth IRAs

In recent years, another option even more advantageous than traditional IRAs, has become available for retirement savers. Roth IRAs allow for tax-free distributions any time after age 59½, provided the taxpayer has had a Roth IRA for at least five years before the initial distribution.

Roth IRA contributions. Unlike traditional IRA contributions, Roth IRA contributions are nondeductible. For 2009, single taxpayers with Modified Adjusted Gross Income (MAGI) of $105,000 or less and married taxpayers who file jointly with MAGI of $166,000 or less can contribute up to $5,000 per year into a Roth IRA. Taxpayers aged 50 and above can also make an additional $1,000 "catch up" contribution each year. Although Roth IRAs do not have a loan feature, per se, any cash contributions made into a Roth IRA may be withdrawn at any time without taxation or penalty, even if the accountholder is under age 59½. However, this type of distribution is irreversible; once the contributions are withdrawn, they cannot be remade. There is no 90-day window during which the accountholder can replenish the funds, as there is with a traditional IRA.

Roth IRA conversions. Another option you have with your TSP is to convert your current plan balance into a Roth IRA instead of rolling it over into a traditional IRA. New rules now allow qualified plan participants to directly roll over their plan balances into a Roth IRA without first having to roll them into a traditional IRA before converting them to a Roth IRA. However, your MAGI cannot exceed $100,000 in the year of conversion. The income realized from the conversion does not count toward this threshold. For example, if your MAGI is $60,000, and you have a TSP balance of $100,000, you can convert the entire $100,000 plan balance. The $100,000 limit applies for both married and single taxpayers. You should note that the Pension Protection Act of 2006

eliminated the income limitation for Roth conversions starting in 2010. However, this provision is subject to possible repeal, so planning a future conversion based on current legislation is risky. Of course, the entire conversion balance is considered taxable ordinary income at the time of conversion. This can, in turn, raise the rate at which other income you receive is taxed, such as wages, Social Security benefits, and investment income. Therefore, participants must carefully consider the income tax ramifications before converting their assets to a Roth IRA and should probably consult with their tax advisors before pursuing this course of action.

Roth IRA distributions. Unlike traditional IRA distributions, Roth IRA distributions do not require mandatory minimum distributions at age 70½. Furthermore, the tax-free status of Roth distributions allows taxpayers to make withdrawals of any size without affecting the taxation of the rest of their assets. The simplicity of Roth distributions also allows less sophisticated taxpayers to handle their finances more easily.

A Roth IRA savings example. The following illustration shows the power of having a large, tax-free pool of cash from which to draw. Suppose you start contributing $5,000 a year to a Roth IRA beginning at age 40. You retire at age 65 and stop making contributions, but allow your Roth to continue to grow for another 5 years. If the investments within your Roth average 10% annual growth over time, then you will have a whopping $870,000 (approximately) in your account by age 70—tax-free. Suppose you want to purchase a vacation home. You need $500,000 to pay for this second home. A distribution from a traditional IRA or qualified plan would immediately result in taxation at the highest marginal tax rate and would also make the maximum amount of your Social Security benefits taxable (85%), if they weren't already. Furthermore, any other income you receive, such as wages from a job, interest and dividend income, or any other type of investment income (except for capital gains) would now be taxed at the highest possible rate as well. But having a Roth IRA effectively prevents your vacation home purchase from infecting the rest of your finances, as the distribution is tax-free and will have no effect on the rate at which your other sources of income are taxed.

Traditional IRAs versus Roth IRAs. Traditional IRAs offer an up-front tax deduction in the year the contribution is made. Roth IRA contributions are nondeductible, but their distributions are tax-free. In many cases, the Roth IRA will provide a greater benefit than the traditional IRA, but not always. There

are many variables that determine which path is better for a given individual, and comparing the two can create a complex equation that may be best performed by your financial planner.

Option 2: A series of monthly payments

If you choose to generate an income while keeping your savings in the TSP, you can elect to receive monthly payments. The monthly payment you choose may be a specific dollar amount, or you can have the TSP calculate a monthly payment based on your life expectancy. Once a year, you can change the amount of your monthly payments. Also, you can ask the TSP to stop monthly payments at any time and have the balance remaining in your account paid to you in a single payment.

Option 3: A life annuity

The difference between monthly payments and annuity payments is that an annuity will pay a monthly benefit to you (or to your survivor) every month for as long as you live. Regular monthly payments will end when your money runs out. Of course, if you choose an annuity, you will no longer have an opportunity to invest your money and benefit from potential future growth.

You can choose to have the TSP purchase an annuity on your behalf from a private insurance company with all or a portion of your account balance. Once an annuity has been purchased, you cannot change your decision. There are three basic types of annuities to consider:

- **A single life annuity** will pay monthly benefits to you during your life only.

- **A joint life annuity with your spouse** will provide income to you while you and your spouse are alive. When one of you dies, annuity payments will continue to be made to the survivor for the rest of his or her life. You may choose either a 50% or 100% payment option for the survivor.

- **A joint life annuity with someone who is not your spouse** pays benefits to you while you and your co-annuitant are alive. When

one of you dies, payments are made to the survivor during his or her life.

The annuity you choose may have other options available. These are explained in the booklet entitled *Withdrawing Your TSP Account After Leaving Federal Service* which can be found at *www.tsp.gov*.

Taxes and your Social Security benefits

In general, all income you receive may be subject to taxes. This includes income from part-time work, money earned during your yard sale, the value of goods or service bartered, distributions from your IRAs, annuity income, and any other income you may have received. In some cases, benefits received from Social Security may be taxed as well. Social Security benefits include monthly retirement, survivor, and disability benefits. Supplemental security income payments are not taxable.

To determine whether your benefits may be taxable, add one-half of your Social Security benefits and all of your other income. If the amount is greater than the base amount for your filing status, then a portion of your benefits will be taxable. To determine the base amount for your filing status, read IRS Publication 554, *Tax Guide for Seniors*.

In general, up to 85% of your benefits may be taxable if:

- The total of one-half of your benefits and all your other income is more than a specific amount ($44,000 for individuals who were married and filing jointly, or $34,000 for single filers), or

- You are married filing separately and lived with your spouse at any time during the year.

This again illustrates the advantage of a Roth IRA, because distributions from a Roth will not affect the taxation of your Social Security benefits, regardless of the size of the distribution.

Tax law is always changing

That's why it is important to remember that the rules may have changed by the time you read this chapter. As a result, the information provided about the ways basic tax rules apply to CSRS and FERS benefits, Thrift Savings Plan payments, and Social Security benefits may no longer be the most current. For this reason, you may want to review some of these resources to get the most up-to-date information about taxes and your benefits:

- **Internal Revenue Service website** at *www.irs.gov*.
  In particular, you may want to review:
  — Publication 554, *Tax Guide for Seniors*
  — Publication 575, *Pension and Annuity Income*

- **Office of Personnel Management website** at *www.OPM.gov*.
  You'll find:
  — Federal Employees Retirement System (FERS) publications
  — Civil Service Retirement System (CSRS) publications
  — Other retirement publications
  — Other retirement resources

- **The Thrift Savings Plan website** at *www.tsp.gov*.

- **The Social Security Online** at *www.ssa.gov*.

Chapter Review

1. What is the Rule of 8?

2. Are FERS and CSRS annuity payments taxable?

3. How would you calculate the amount of an annuity benefit that is taxable?

4. Name three types of distribution options from the TSP. Which do you think is the best option?

5. Will your Social Security benefits be taxable? How will that affect your retirement income?

Big Mistake #8

Failing to calculate the benefits and costs of paying or repaying for prior government service

You may have an opportunity to pay or repay any amounts you have withdrawn or have been refunded to you from your annuity. There generally are three kinds of service credit payments:

- **Payments for non-deduction service**—to cover a period of service that may be creditable for retirement, but for which no retirement deductions were withheld from your salary.

- **Repayments of refunded CSRS and FERS contributions**—to cover a period of service during which CSRS or FERS deductions were withheld but later refunded.

- **Post-1956 military service credit payment**—to cover post-1956 military service which can only be credited when a payment is made to the retirement fund. Under CSRS, a deposit is not needed if you do not qualify for Social Security benefits at retirement.

If you are eligible to make payments or repayments, you may be able to claim or reclaim credit for prior service. Repayment can increase your creditable service hours, the amount of your annuity, and your Social Security benefits.

There is a right answer to the question of whether you should pay or repay for prior government service. As you consider whether to make a payment or repayment, ask yourself: How long do I need to live to get the money back in increased annuity payments?

*Retiring rich: Is it dollars in an account
or a predictable future income?*

Chapter 9
The Logistics
of Retirement

You're celebrating the holidays with family. Talk turns to retirement. Your brother-in-law, Bob, who is about your age and has worked for a large public company for years, starts talking about how much money he has tucked away in various retirement savings accounts. You are impressed by the amount of money he has saved. You feel that green monster, Envy, tickling your brain... but just brush it away. When push comes to shove, your retirement will probably be very similar to Bob's. What will be different is your cash flow.

Imagine you and Bob retire at age 65 and you both live for 25 years in retirement. Let's assume you will retire with 30 years of government service and receive a $50,000 annual pension. When Bob retires, he also would like to have an annual income of $50,000. He will invest his savings conservatively with 25% of his savings in stocks (to keep pace with inflation), 40% in bonds, and 35% in cash or short-term alternatives. To generate an income of about $50,000 each year, and to have a 90% certainty that his savings will last for 25 years, Bob will need to have $1.1 million saved and invested for retirement.[1] A $50,000 annuity is roughly the equivalent of $1 million plus in savings. That's why you work for Uncle Sam—you want to retire rich.

Embracing the retirement process

In my office, the end of the year and the beginning of the New Year are remarkably busy. Why? It is because many, many people decide to retire from government during the last quarter of the year. As a result, the government processes retirement applications more slowly, and when problems arise, issues get resolved far less quickly than at other times of the year.

The best advice I can give you about retiring from the government is to plan ahead. Be proactive. If you want to work for Uncle Sam and retire rich, you need to give yourself enough lead time to ensure your retirement will be all you want it to be. As you have learned in earlier chapters, there are lots of pieces to align properly to ensure your retirement date, income, and benefits coverage all meet your expectations.

So, how can you ensure you'll have all that (or as close to it as possible)? Start planning long before your retirement date draws near. If you know you're a procrastinator, or if the demands of family and work may prevent you from planning effectively, enlist the help of a professional financial planner. He or she can help keep you on track to reach your retirement goals.

Five years before retirement

It's a good idea to embrace the retirement process at least five years before you plan to retire. Why? Your insurance coverage—health and life—must be in place for at least five years before you retire if you plan to carry that coverage into retirement. Order a copy of the pamphlet called *Checklist for Health Benefits and Life Insurance Coverage* from the Office of Personnel Management. It is intended for employees who are planning for retirement and will provide detailed information about how to qualify for life, health, and long-term care benefits.

Remember, health coverage is a very big deal. According to Ameriprise, today health care costs average $9,000 per retiree per year, and that estimate was based on mid-range coverage costs for Medicare premiums and deductibles, Medigap insurance, long-term care insurance, and other health-care insurance.[2]

As a government employee, you have a tremendous advantage over private sector employees. More and more private sector employers are discontinuing health coverage for retired workers. When it is available, the costs generally

are very high. As a government employee, if you plan ahead, you can carry your health insurance, long-term care insurance, and life insurance coverage into retirement for a reasonable cost.

Confirm your plan and retirement income

In addition to ensuring you'll have the coverage you need after you retire, it's a good idea to make sure you are on track to hit your retirement income target. The first step is to confirm you are participating in the correct plan. Some of the worst retirement mix-ups have occurred when individuals are informed, after applying for retirement, they've been participating in CSRS when they really qualified for FERS. The effect is that the retiree's income is far less than expected, and he or she may not have time, or the will, to set aside additional savings.

You'll also want to estimate the income you'll receive from your pension. Will it provide you with the standard of living you expected? Will you need to save a bit more in the TSP, or in other accounts, so that you can provide a higher level of supplemental income to your annuity? It's my hope that you begin considering these questions many years before your retirement. The review at five years should confirm your expectations and give you a chance to tweak your results.

Decide whether to make service credit deposits

You may have an opportunity to make service credit deposits to increase your annual annuity payments. There are a number of different kinds of payments, including deposits for non-deduction of service, re-deposits of refunded contributions, and military service credit deposits (for service completed after 1956). You should discuss deposit options and the benefits with the OPM or a financial planning professional. This is a highly technical area, but deposits can make a significant difference in the amount of income you'll receive during retirement.

Sign up for pre-retirement counseling

The Office of Personnel Management may offer pre-retirement counseling. A counselor will confirm that you are eligible to retire on the date you have in mind (or that you are not), as well as review your eligibility to keep health, life,

and long-term care insurance coverage as a retiree. You can also discuss service credit deposits. Have your counselor identify any information that may be missing from your personnel folder. It is essential that your folder be complete when you apply for retirement. Missing information can delay the processing of your retirement application.

With five years to go you'll want to:

- Ask for an estimate of your annuity benefits.

- Ask for a list verifying periods of civilian and military service.

- Verify that you will meet the age, service, and other requirements necessary to retire on your desired retirement date.

- Ensure your personnel folder accurately documents your current FEHB and FEGLI coverage. (Check to make sure your current plan options are correctly identified.)

- Make sure your beneficiaries are correct.

- Determine whether you are eligible to receive Social Security benefits.

One year before retirement

Retirement is almost upon you. That last year can pass faster than you ever dreamed was possible. Ask for a copy of the *Checklist for Employees Preparing to Retire*. Read through it and mark key tasks and dates on your calendar so you do not forget a step. Here are some important steps to take:

Review your official personnel folder

Start the countdown to retirement by requesting a copy of your personnel folder from the Office of Personnel Management. This is the central repository for all of the records the federal government has regarding your service. Your folder should include the beginning and ending dates for each period of employment that will be included in calculating your benefits, as well as promotion and pay increase dates that will be used to figure your "high-three" average salary, and other service information that could affect the amount of your pension income. If you discover that any of your service has not been verified or any of the

required documentation is missing, ask the Office of Personnel Management for assistance immediately.

Request an updated retirement benefits estimate

At this point an updated retirement benefits estimate should be very close to the actual amount you will receive from your annuity. You should also collect the most recent information you have, or request updated information, about any other sources of income you'll rely on during retirement. Take some time for a reality check. Will your annuity, savings from the TSP, Social Security benefits (if you are eligible for them), and your other savings provide you with enough income to live comfortably throughout your retirement? If not, you may need to delay your retirement.

Review your survivor benefit options

If your annuity income needs to last throughout your lifetime and that of your spouse, you need to understand the eligibility requirements for survivor benefits and how much they will cost. If you want your spouse to receive less than full benefits, his or her consent is required. It is important to remember that spouses who are not covered by your annuity do not have the right to continue Federal Employees Health Benefits (FEHB) coverage when you die.

Verify your ability to carry your benefits coverage into retirement

Check on health care and life insurance. If you won't meet the five-year requirement by your planned retirement date, you may want to delay your retirement. Remember, you must be enrolled when you retire and retire on an immediate annuity.

Choose your retirement date

CSRS annuities can begin on the first, second, or third day of the month. However, FERS annuities can only begin on the first day of a month.

Contact the Social Security office

If you are eligible for Social Security benefits or Medicare, contact the Social Security Administration to apply for benefits. You can visit a Social Security office, call Social Security, or visit their website at *www.ssa.gov.*

Complete an application for retirement

You are finally ready to initiate your separation from government service. After your application for retirement has been received by the Office of Personnel Management Retirement Operations Center, Office of Retirement Programs, you will receive an acknowledgment and a retirement claim number. The claim number includes the letters "CSA" (Civil Service Annuity). Do not lose it. You will need it any time you communicate with the Office of Personnel Management about your claim.

It's possible your application for retirement may not be accepted. One of the great reasons to work for the government is that you have wonderful job security. The downside is that, if you are serving an essential function, you may not be able to retire when you would like to retire.

Entering retirement

The Office of Personnel Management will send you a booklet summarizing your retirement information as soon as your claim has been completed. The booklet will provide information about your average salary, "high-three" average income, benefits coverage, tax issues, cost of living increases, and much more. Review the booklet thoroughly and contact the Office of Personnel Management using the methods provided if you have questions.

Interim payments

One of the very best reasons to apply for retirement early is to provide the Office of Personnel Management with enough time to process your claim before you retire. If you wait until the last quarter of the year to apply, there's a good chance you will receive interim annuity payments for some period after you separate from service. Interim annuity payments usually pay about 85%

to 95% of your anticipated regular monthly payment annuity payment, after deductions for benefits coverage.

You can expect to receive interim payments until your claim has been processed and completed. So if you apply for retirement during peak times when processing may be slower, you may enter retirement with less income than you anticipated. Don't worry. You will be paid the difference between what was paid to you and what should have been paid to you. You just won't receive it until your claim is completed.

Your TSP account

You will receive a TSP withdrawal package from your agency after you retire. The distribution option you choose can have a profound affect on the value of the wealth you've accumulated in the TSP, so it's a good idea to work with a financial professional to ensure you make sound choices. You can make a TSP withdrawal election after you leave service. Just submit Form TSP-70, *Request for Full Withdrawal*, to the TSP Service Office.

Your voluntary contribution account (CSRS employees)

Once you have separated from service, you can request a refund of the savings in your voluntary contribution account. Just complete Form RI 38-124, *Voluntary Contributions Election*, and send it to the Office of Personnel Management.

Resources

If you have questions about retirement, you can call the Office of Personnel Management or visit their website at *www.opm.gov*. You'll find a wealth of information, as well as up-to-date addresses and phone numbers. In addition to contacting the Office of Personnel Management, you may also want to contact:

Thrift Savings Plan:
>   1-877-968-3778
>   1-877-847-4385 (TDD)
>   1-404-233-4400 (International, not toll-free)

Social Security Administration:
> 1-800-772-1213
> 1-800-325-0778 (TDD)

Medicare:
> 1-800-633-4227

Federal Long-term Care Insurance Program:
> 1-800-582-3337
> 1-800-843-3557 (TDD)

Internal Revenue Service:
> 1-800-829-1040 (General tax information)
> 1-800-829-4059 (General tax information–TDD)
> 1-800-829-3676 (Publications and forms)

Chapter Review

1. When should you begin planning for retirement?

2. How long must you be enrolled in benefits coverage (life and health) to carry coverage into retirement?

3. What type of annuity will you receive? Will it provide enough income for you to retire comfortably?

Notes

[1] *Retirement Income Calculator.* T. Rowe Price. Web. 28 Oct. 2009. <http://www3.troweprice.com/ric/ric/public/ric.do>.

[2] *Anticipate Retirement Health Costs.* Ameriprise Financial. Web. 28 Oct. 2009. <http://retirement.ameriprise.com/planning-for-retirement/retirement-income-funds/retirement-cost.asp>.

Big Mistake #9

Not planning for the effects of the Windfall Elimination Provision, Government Pension Offset, and Social Security earnings limitation rules

When you receive your estimated benefits statement from Social Security each year, it may make you feel pretty confident you'll retire rich. With a civil service pension and Social Security benefits, you'll have more income than you ever dreamed, right? Wrong. Millions of beneficiaries have had their benefits reduced because of the:

Windfall Elimination Provision (WEP): If you're a CSRS annuitant, your Social Security benefits will probably be significantly less than the amount shown on your benefits estimate due to the WEP. It all depends on the size of your annuity and the amount of your benefits. The good news is that the reduction in Social Security benefits cannot exceed 50% of your annuity benefit. The bad news is that it can be as much as a 50% reduction. For more information go to *http://www.ssa.gov/pubs/10045.html*.

Government Pension Offset (GPO): If you're a CSRS annuitant and you're eligible to receive survivor benefits from Social Security, your Social Security benefits will be reduced based on the amount of your CSRS annuity due to the GPO. There is no good news here. Your Social Security benefit can be reduced by 100%. For more information go to *http://www.ssa.gov/retirez/gpo.htm*.

Retirement Earnings Test: If you continue working after you apply for Social Security, your benefits may be reduced. If you are younger than full retirement age, there is a limit to how much you can earn and still receive full Social Security benefits. If you are younger than full retirement age during all of 2009, you must deduct $1 from your benefits for each $2 you earned above $14,160. This figure is normally adjusted for inflation each year. You can have your financial planner calculate an estimate of the reduction and its impact on your cash flow.

Chapter 10
The Changing Face of Retirement

Planning for retirement is becoming more challenging each year. Health care costs are increasing, people are living longer, and private pension plans are disappearing. As a federal government employee, you have significant advantages over many private sector workers. By planning properly, you can retire with far fewer worries than many of your private sector brethren. Most private sector workers are responsible for saving, investing their savings properly, and then managing those assets so they don't run out of money during their retirements. You contribute to an annuity and receive a guaranteed lifetime income in return. In addition, you have an opportunity to accumulate additional savings and receive health care, long-term care, and life insurance benefits during retirement.

You have an opportunity to retire rich! If you take the time to understand the rules that guide the government programs available to you—or work with a financial planner who understands them—you can expect to retire with:

- **A generous pension income from Uncle Sam**. CSRS participants can generally expect to receive about 55% to 65% of their "high three" average pay. FERS participants can generally expect to receive about 25% to 30% of their "high-three" average pay.

- **Social Security benefits for FERS participants**. If you participate in FERS, you will be able to collect Social Security benefits. Your combined annuity and Social Security benefits may provide post-retirement income comparable to that received by CSRS participants.

- **A nest egg of tax-deferred savings with the Thrift Savings Plan (TSP)**. The TSP provides CSRS and FERS employees with an opportunity to set aside savings outside their annuities. The government will match contributions made by FERS participants, allowing them to save more, faster. If you save in the TSP, you defer paying taxes on those savings, and on any earnings on those savings, until you withdraw them from your account. Your TSP nest egg can provide extra income during retirement.

- **Health care coverage**. Under the FEHB program, the federal government pays up to 75% of the cost of your health benefits coverage—and your family's—even after retirement. That's a perk that is becoming increasingly rare in the private sector.

- **Long-term care coverage—no questions asked**. Federal employees, retirees, active members of the Uniformed Services, and qualified family members can purchase long-term care insurance through the Federal LTC Insurance Program. One of the most significant advantages of the program is that you don't have to answer health questions during open enrollment periods.

- **A variety of life insurance options**. Life insurance benefits are available to government employees through FEGLI during retirement—as long as you meet some basic requirements.

Make the most of your retirement

Having advantages and options is wonderful—especially when it comes to saving and investing for retirement—but it's not enough. In order to retire rich, you need to make a plan for your retirement. Once you have developed a plan, you'll need to review it whenever your personal situation changes. If you get married or divorced, have children, receive an inheritance, or experience another type of life-changing event, you may need to adjust your plan.

Talk with your spouse

The first step in planning is to talk with your spouse. A recent survey found that 382% of baby boomer married couples don't agree on any retirement basic: retirement age, working in retirement, or retirement lifestyle![1]

Determine how much you need to save and invest

Once you and your spouse have aligned your expectations, it's time to prepare, plan, and persevere. If you haven't already, it's a good idea to develop a net worth statement. Decide how much income you need to live well during retirement. Think about the effect inflation may have on your retirement income needs. Then determine how much you will need to have in personal savings to supplement your pension income and any income you may receive from Social Security. If you save in the TSP—and you probably should—you'll want to carefully consider the options for investing your savings. Evaluate your risk tolerance and time frame—and remember the importance of choosing a diversified portfolio of investments.

Understand the rules applicable to Social Security benefits

If you qualify to receive Social Security—perhaps you worked in the private sector at one time—make sure you are familiar with the Windfall Elimination Provision and the Government Pension Offset, which are discussed in Chapter 7, so that you do not overestimate your potential retirement income. If you fall into that trap, you may end up retiring with far less income than you expected.

Know how income taxes will affect your retirement income

A common expectation is that retirees will pay less in taxes because they'll be in a lower tax bracket after they retire. Today, there are just a few tax brackets, and each one covers a broad range of income. Unless you are very close to the baseline income for a tax bracket, it's unlikely you'll be in a lower bracket after you retire.

It's also important to work with a tax professional to understand the way in which your government annuity benefits will be taxed. You should understand federal tax rules and also consider state taxes. If you're considering relocating after retirement, you should familiarize yourself with state tax laws. There are ten states that exempt government annuities from taxation, and seven states don't assess any income taxes.

Also, there is a variety of distribution options for any savings you've accumulated in a TSP account. Make sure you evaluate those options carefully and

thoroughly understand the effect each could have on your tax situation before you take a distribution.

Review your plan continuously

Once you have a plan in place, you'll need to review your plan every few years or as your income changes. As retirement draws closer, you'll want to begin pre-retirement planning. Start *at least* five years before you plan to retire. The Office of Personnel Management Web site at *www.opm.gov/retire/* provides an excellent timeline for pre-retirement planning. Thoroughly review the various retirement options available to you before you make a decision about when to retire, and make certain you will be able to meet the eligibility requirements for your preferred option.

Avoid the BIG mistakes

In each chapter of this book, I've covered some key mistakes government employees make. They include:

1. *Not understanding the effects of inflation and long life expectancies.*

2. *Not having a comprehensive financial plan.*

3. *Not having an estate plan.*

4. *Purchasing a fixed income annuity option.*

5. *Using the wrong investment methodology.*

6. *Choosing incorrect types and amounts of insurance.*

7. *Not having a plan to address long-term care expenses.*

8. *Failing to calculate the benefits and costs of paying or repaying for prior government service.*

9. *Not planning for the effects of WEP, GPO, and Social Security earnings limitation rules.*

10. *Choosing the wrong survivorship option.*

Prepare and you can retire rich!

In earlier chapters, you learned about the tools and resources available to you as a government employee, as well as various processes and procedures you need to follow in order to maximize your retirement income and benefits. I strongly suggest you develop a relationship with a financial planning professional who has experience working with government employees who can help you develop a sound financial plan that includes saving, investing, and risk management. If you follow the suggestions in this book, make informed choices about the benefits available to you, set aside additional savings, and avoid the big mistakes that can derail retirement, you'll be on your way to retiring rich!

Notes

[1] Fidelity Investments. "2009 Fidelity Investments Couples Retirement Study: Executive Summary." Fidelity Brokerage Services, LLC. Web. 28 Oct. 2009. <http://www2.prnewswire.com/mnr/fidelity/38691/docs/38691-NEWExecSum_Couples2009_060509FINAL.pdf>.

Big Mistake #**10**

Choosing the wrong survivorship option

At retirement, government employees with eligible dependents have the privilege *and* the obligation to choose survivorship benefits for their benefits plans. Survivor annuities replace income for surviving family members, and if the beneficiary is your spouse, benefits generally are paid for life. Children qualify for survivor annuities if they are younger than age 18 and unmarried. If you have a child who is disabled, he or she may qualify for a survivor annuity beyond age 18. Importantly, having a survivor annuity will allow family members to be covered by FEHB after your death, as long as you were in a family plan when you died.

So what's the catch? There is a cost when you elect a survivorship option. For CSRS employees, if you choose a full survivor benefit of 55%, your retirement annuity will be reduced by 10%. If you're covered under FERS, the maximum survivor benefit is 50% and the cost is 10% of your original annuity amount. FERS employees may elect one survivor annuity option of either 50% or 25% of their full annuity. CSRS employees can elect a percentage or a specific dollar amount. (If a dollar amount is elected, it can be as small as $1.)

Epilogue:
Welcome to the Final Frontier

While this book is dedicated to exploring the various technical aspects of government retirement plans, I feel compelled to cover one final issue that will materially impact your life once you stop working.

As I briefly mentioned earlier, modern retirees can often expect to live relatively healthy, functional lives for at least 10 years after they stop working. However, this improvement in both the length and quality of life has brought with it a new psychological frontier that must be traversed as well. Unlike your parents, you will most likely face an extended period of normal living after you leave your job.

After you have stopped working, you may be surprised at how much you have to redefine your sense of identity and who you are as a person. Many employees and workers, particularly successful ones, base much of their sense of worth on what they do for a living. Retirement can effectively yank the foundation out from under this mindset.

For most of your life, retirement probably stood as a far-off goal that you would seemingly never reach. Then, suddenly, your entire life is rearranged, and any previous failure in preparation becomes immediately apparent. Furthermore, the realization crashes in that no further work goals will be accomplished, and the last rung of your ladder has been climbed. This adjustment will take time to digest, and it may not go down easily, especially for those who failed to accomplish what they desired professionally. In fact, for many retirees, retirement is

a downright frightening proposition, not only financially if they do not have adequate resources to support themselves, but also emotionally. When you were in school, you went to class for part of the day and then had the rest of the day to yourself. During your working years, you worked from Monday to Friday and then had the weekend to yourself. But now, you are finished working and have the entire rest of your *life* to yourself.

Of course, the financial media has been no help at all in resolving this issue. While the financial industry has done everything in its power to provide actual products and services for every financial situation conceivable, most of the visual material in this arena promotes a fantasy world, a world that has no widows, divorces, loneliness, continuing job requirements, or medical issues. There is an implicit assumption that a successful retirement is simply a matter of making the right arrangements and having the right attitudes, that there is nothing to fear, that retirement is something anyone can manage with just a little common sense.

This assumption creates much confusion between the business of arranging for retirement versus the actual experience of becoming a retired person. With the underpinnings of work and family removed, retirement can demand new answers from its participants concerning such questions as, "Who am I? Do I have a focus? How should I spend my time? Can I now cope with the future?" These can be scary questions for retirees who may, for the first time in their lives, have meaningful choices regarding time, place, and purpose with no map or script.

Transitioning

The immediate transition from work to retirement can be a time of major psychological upheaval for many retirees. Most workers spend their lives looking forward to a happy retirement, but when it finally comes, they often discover it is much different from what they expected. In her book *For Better or For Worse, but Not for Lunch,* Dr. Sara Yogev outlines six separate phases in the retirement adjustment process:

- **Preretirement**–Plans and attitudes about retirement are formed during the working years.

- **Retirement Event**–This is the actual cessation of employment and is often accompanied by some sort of celebration.

- **Honeymoon Phase**–Just as in marriage, this is the initial phase of bliss that occurs right after the event, where all of the initial trips, fun, and projects that have been planned are executed.

- **Disenchantment**–This phase, which follows the honeymoon, encompasses the almost inevitable letdown many feel after the initial elation of retirement wears off.

- **Reorientation**–This is the subsequent process of adjustment and coping that must be made in order to adapt to current circumstances.

- **Routine**–This is the final order of life that comes about after the adjustments have been made.

The period from retirement until life becomes routine may not be a good time for you to make permanent, long-term financial decisions, such as whether to move to Florida or buy a lake home. This is also typically the phase where most retirees must deal with the loss of identity that came from their jobs. For some retirees (such as low-income workers who performed manual labor or other tedious work), this may not be much of an issue. But for someone who was a Senior Vice President for a multinational corporation, this sudden loss of status can be a major emotional factor to deal with.

For example, as a government employee, you probably became accustomed to a daily, weekly, and monthly routine you could count on to structure your future plans around. You probably derived at least a measure of satisfaction and recognition from your work, at least from your co-workers.

Relationship issues

Perhaps no other area of life will be so affected by your retirement as your relationship with your spouse or significant other. Because retirement can cause the focus on one's primary relationship to intensify greatly, it is possible for issues that have been bubbling under the surface for years or even decades to suddenly surface.

During your working years, you may have made an unspoken emotional pact that must finally be revised. In some marriages, the pact may consist of the husband's emotional needs taking a backseat to the children while he gives first priority to work, and the wife's emotional needs taking a backseat to the demands of her job, domestic duties, or both while the children are at home. But retirement can expose the problems inherent in this arrangement and much resentment from both partners over past unmet needs may erupt when the necessary time suddenly becomes available to meet those needs.

Other issues also come to the forefront at retirement. Over 3 million families have grandparents raising grandchildren, and grandparenting styles must be considered. Whether to move to another location is another important issue that must be resolved. But regardless of where a couple decides to live, there are several domestic and relational issues to contend with.

A new balance must be found between separateness and togetherness. Retirement causes some people to "cling" to their partners, while some don't attach enough importance to maintaining their personal social routines and autonomy. Those who have worked outside the home for years can feel uncomfortable hanging around the house all day, and those who have stayed at home may feel their partners are intruding on their "territory."

Logistically, there can be substantial benefits when one partner retires before the other, or when both retire at the same time. Women who continue to work after their partners retire often have lower marital satisfaction than others due to deviation from traditional male-female roles and greater opportunities to contest the unfair division of domestic labor. As stated previously, retirement brings couples face to face with no traditional escape mechanisms. Spending more time together can throw a harsher light on a partner's annoying habits, and men are more likely to become depressed as a result of loss of autonomy, while women tend to get more depressed as a result of family problems.

Psychological aspects of aging

Of course, on top of the emotional issues that come with retirement, retirees must also contend with the physical and psychological aspects of aging. Historically speaking, it must be understood that when Social Security was

created in 1935, those aged 65 and over were considered old. There was only one category of old, and anyone much over the age of 50 belonged in it, without exception.

But today, modern gerontology has subcategorized the elderly into three groups:

- The "young-old" (age 65 to 74)

- The "old-old" (age 75 to 84)

- The "oldest-old" (age 85 and up)

Nowadays, those in the first category are often healthy and functional, while those in the second category tend to more closely resemble the traditional definition of old in terms of health. Of course, the final category encompasses the truly aged (and often infirm).

While many retirees enjoy a period of reasonable health and functionality upon retirement, the physical and mental decline that inevitably accompanies aging also takes an emotional toll. Depression is a major symptom afflicting many retirees. The losses that accompany old age, such as loss of job, social status, and independence have been cited as major factors leading to this condition. These factors also come at a time when the retiree is less able to cope with them, thus compounding the problem. But depression is clearly not a normal symptom of aging, and therefore must be treated accordingly.

From a less clinical perspective, retirement can also be a time of reflection where one is forced to come to terms with many things previously undealt with. While this issue was discussed previously in relation to work, it also applies in other areas of life as well. For some, a key issue may be coming to terms with past failures that cannot be rectified or unfulfilled dreams and desires that will never materialize.

Others may have physical issues intrude into their psyches. For example, a retiree with a very strong independent streak may no longer be able to function on his or her own; this state of continual neediness can be extremely difficult to accept. As referenced previously, this period generally does not begin as soon as it used to. In times past, the physical onset of old age usually began at or near retirement, with little or no period of simultaneous health and freedom to be enjoyed. While a detailed exploration of the

physical aspects of aging is beyond the scope of this book, this issue will assuredly impact retirees both financially and psychologically, as increased medical and prescription drug care is needed and retirees come to grips with their mortality and physical limitations.

A key issue for retirees to focus on is the ability to separate retirement from old age. *Retirement* is an event, and *old age* is a process, state of mind, or both. All retirees know that they are growing older, of course, but they do not necessarily know when they grow old. This confusion stems from the circumstances of previous retired generations, where retirement and old age were almost always congruent.

Coping strategies

Earlier we listed some of the characteristics possessed by those who successfully transition into retirement. Here, Dr. Sara Yogev outlines 10 steps to a better retirement:

- Say goodbye to work.
- Share expectations.
- Address your relationship with money.
- Prepare for mixed feelings.
- Address issues as they surface.
- Custom design your schedule.
- Stay mentally active.
- Give your spouse or significant other physical and emotional space.
- Celebrate your sexuality.
- Celebrate your body.

Gradually easing into retirement, perhaps by shifting from full-time to part-time work, can soften both the financial and psychological blow. Anything that can be done to prevent an all-or-nothing transition can be helpful in easing the process. It is important for retirees to learn how to be patient,

understand their changes, let go of the past, search for the future, and then create their new lives.

C. Melody Edmondson identifies several different types of retirement personalities:

- **Continuers** are retirees for whom identity in previous work is central.

- **Adventurers** do more in new directions, paid or unpaid.

- **Searchers** are those who are separating from their past but haven't found a new (temporal) place yet.

- **Easy gliders** are content, go with the flow, and enjoy retirement.

- **Retreaters** have given up on forging a new, rewarding life.

Ultimately, activity, diversity, and connection with others are among the hallmarks of fulfilling lives in retirement. Activities should provide a sense of achievement, preferably public. Ideally, at least some of them should be "real life" ventures, and not just hobbies or personal tasks. In fact, having an element of risk present may increase satisfaction, especially for men.

Glossary
of Financial Terms

Adjusted Gross Income (AGI) – An interim calculation in the computation of income tax liability. It is computed by subtracting certain allowable adjustments from gross income.

Administrator – A person appointed by the court to settle an estate when there is no will.

After-Tax Return – The return from an investment after the effects of taxes have been taken into account.

Alternative Form of Annuity – Retirees who have a life-threatening illness or other critical medical condition can choose to receive an Alternative Form of Annuity. In the alternative annuity, you receive a reduced monthly benefit, plus a lump sum payment equal to all your unrefunded contributions to the retirement fund. The amount of reduction in your monthly benefit depends on your age at the time you retire and the amount of your retirement contributions. Your election of an Alternative Form of Annuity does not affect the potential survivor annuity payable to your spouse or children.

Alternative Minimum Tax – A method of calculating income tax that disallows certain deductions, credits, and exclusions. This was intended to ensure that individuals, trusts, and estates that benefit from tax preferences do not escape all federal income tax liability. People must calculate their taxes both ways and pay the greater of the two amounts.

Annuitant – A former employee entitled to an annuity under a retirement system established for employees. This includes the retirement system of a non-appropriated fund instrumentality of the Department of Defense or the Coast Guard.

Annuity Starting Date – For most types of annuities, the first day of the month following either the date after the day you separate from service or the date after your last day in pay, whichever is earlier. If you were in pay status for three days or less in the month of your retirement, the annuity starting date is the date after either the day you separated from service or your last day in pay and in which you meet age and service requirements, whichever is earlier.

Asset Allocations – The process of repositioning assets within a portfolio to maximize return for a given level of risk. This process is usually done using the historical performance of the asset classes within sophisticated mathematical models.

Asset – Anything owned that has monetary value.

Asset Class – A category of investments with similar characteristics.

Audit – The examination of the accounting and financial documents of a firm by an objective professional. The audit is done to determine the records' accuracy, consistency, and conformity to legal and accounting principles.

Basic Insurance – The coverage, based on your annual rate of basic pay, which you automatically have as an eligible employee unless you waive it.

Basic Insurance Amount – The amount of Basic insurance on which you pay premiums. It is determined by taking your annual rate of basic pay, rounding it up to the next higher thousand (if not already an even thousand dollar amount), and adding $2,000.

Bear Market – When the stock market appears to be declining overall, it is said to be a bear market.

Beneficiary – A person named in a life insurance policy, annuity, will, trust, or other agreement to receive a financial benefit upon the death of the owner. A beneficiary can be an individual, company, organization, and so on.

Blue Chip Stock – The common stock of a company with a long history of profitability and consistent dividend payments.

Bond – A bond is evidence of a debt in which the issuer promises to pay the bondholders a specified amount of interest and to repay the principal at maturity. Bonds are usually issued in multiples of $1,000.

Book Value – The net value of a company's assets, less its liabilities and the liquidation price of its preferred issues. The net asset value divided by the number of shares of common stock outstanding equals the book value per share, which may be higher or lower than the stock's market value.

Bull Market – When the stock market appears to be advancing overall, it is said to be a bull market.

Buy-Sell Agreement – A buy-sell agreement is an arrangement between two or more parties that obligates one party to buy the business and another party to sell the business upon the death, disability, or retirement of one of the owners.

Capital Gain or Loss – The difference between the sales price and the purchase price of a capital asset. When that difference is positive, the difference is referred to as a capital gain. When the difference is negative, it is a capital loss.

Cash Equivalents – Short-term investments, such as U.S. Treasury securities, certificates of deposit, and money market fund shares which can be readily converted into cash.

Cash Surrender Value – The amount that an insurance policyholder is entitled to receive when he or she discontinues coverage. Policyholders are usually able to borrow against the surrender value of a policy from the insurance company.

Catch-up Contributions – Additional retirement plan contributions that can be made by governmental (and non-governmental) employees age 50 and older to help bolster their retirement savings. These contributions are intended to be a partial remedy for workers who could not afford to save for retirement earlier in their lives, and who therefore need to contribute more than the maximum amount to accumulate a sufficient nest egg.

Certified Financial Planner™(CFP®) – A designation granted by the CFP® Board of Standards (Washington, DC) to individuals who complete a comprehensive curriculum in financial planning, pass a written examination, and have qualifying experience. This curriculum includes risk management, tax planning, employee benefits, investments, and estate planning.

Certified Public Accountant (CPA) – A professional license granted by a state board of accountancy to an individual who has passed the Uniform CPA Examination (administered by the American Institute of Certified Public Accountants) and has fulfilled that state's educational and professional experience requirements for certification.

Charitable Lead Trust – A trust established for the benefit of a charitable organization under which the charitable organization receives income from an asset for a set number of years or for the trustor's lifetime. Upon the termination of the trust, the asset reverts to the trustor or to his or her designated heirs. This type of trust reduces estate taxes and allows the heirs to retain control of the assets.

Charitable Remainder Trust – A trust established for the benefit of a charitable organization under which the trustor receives income from an asset for a set number of years or for the trustor's lifetime. Upon the termination of the trust, the asset reverts to the charitable organization. The trustor receives a charitable contribution deduction in the year in which the trust is established and is exempted from capital gains tax on the assets placed in the trust.

Chartered Financial Consultant (ChFC) – A designation granted by the American College (Bryn Mawr, PA) to individuals who pass a series of written examinations on topics related to financial services, taxation, economics, and estate planning.

Chartered Life Underwriter (CLU) – A designation granted by the American College (Bryn Mawr, PA) to individuals who pass a series of written examinations on topics related to insurance, taxation, economics, and estate planning.

Child – As used in the definition of family member (Basic Insurance for Option C): natural child, adopted child, or step-child or foster child who lives with you in a regular parent-child relationship. Stillborn children are not eligible.

The Civil Service Retirement System (CSRS) – See *CSRS*.

COBRA – The Consolidated Omnibus Budget Reconciliation Act is a federal law requiring employers with more than 20 employees to offer terminated or retired employees the opportunity to continue their health insurance coverage for 18 months at the employee's expense. Coverage may be extended to the employee's dependents for 36 months in the case of divorce or death of the employee.

Coinsurance or Co-Payment – The amount an insured person pays for a covered medical and/or dental expense if his or her insurance doesn't provide 100% coverage.

Commodities – The generic term for goods such as grains, foodstuffs, livestock, oil, and metals that are traded on national exchanges. These exchanges deal in both "spot" trading (for current delivery) and "futures" trading (for delivery in future months).

Common Stock – A unit of ownership in a corporation. Common stockholders participate in the corporation's profits or losses by receiving dividends and by capital gains or losses in the stock's share price.

Community Property – State laws vary, but generally all property acquired during a marriage—excluding property one spouse receives from an inheritance or gift—is considered community property, and each partner is entitled to one half. This includes debt accumulated. There are currently nine community property states: Arizona, California, Idaho, Louisiana, Nevada, New Mexico, Texas, Washington, and Wisconsin.

Compound Interest – Interest that is computed on the principal and on the accrued interest. Compound interest may be computed continuously, daily, monthly, quarterly, semiannually, or annually.

Consumer Price Index – The U. S. Department of Labor's main indicator of inflation. The Consumer Price Index is calculated each month from the cost of some 400 retail items in urban areas throughout the United States.

Coverdell Education Savings Account (formerly known as an Education IRA) – A college savings program in which people can contribute up to $2,000 per year for students under age 18. Income eligibility limits apply.

CSRS – The Civil Service Retirement System. The retirement plan offered to federal employees before 1984. This plan was considerably more generous than FERS

Credit Risk – The chance of default and subsequent failure to make interest and principal payments for a bond or other debt security.

Creditable Service – Service provided to the government by an employee that counts toward retirement benefit calculations. Creditable service can include

intermittent service, short breaks in service, worker's compensation time, and other types of service.

Deduction – An amount that can be subtracted from gross income, from a gross estate, or from a gift thereby lowering the amount on which tax is assessed.

Defined Benefit Plan – A qualified retirement plan under which a retiring employee will receive a guaranteed retirement fund usually payable in install-ments. Annual contributions may be made to the plan by the employer at the level needed to fund the benefit. The annual contributions are limited to a specified amount, indexed to inflation.

Defined Contribution Plan – A qualified retirement plan under which the annual contributions made by the employer or employee are generally stated as a fixed percentage of the employee's compensation or company profits. The amount of retirement benefits is not guaranteed; rather, it depends upon the investment performance of the employee's account.

Deposit – A deposit is the payment of the retirement deductions, plus inter-est, that would have been withheld from your pay if you had been covered by the Civil Service Retirement System (CSRS) or Federal Employees Re-tirement System (FERS) during a period of employment when retirement deductions were not withheld from your salary. You are not required to make this type of payment.

Diversification – Investing in different companies, industries, or asset classes. Diversification may also mean the participation of a large corporation in a wide range of business activities.

Dividend – A pro rata portion of earnings distributed in cash by a corpora-tion to its stockholders. In preferred stock, dividends are usually fixed; with common shares, dividends may vary with the fortunes of the company.

Dollar Cost Averaging – A system of investing in which the investor buys a fixed dollar amount of securities at regular intervals. The investor thus buys more shares when the price is low and fewer shares when it rises, and the aver-age cost per share is lower than the average price per share.

EE Bond – A type of U.S. Savings Bond that pays a set rate of interest and is issued at a discount and matures at par. EE bonds reach face value in 20 years but will continue paying interest for another 10 years.

Efficient Frontier – A statistical result from the analysis of the risk and return for a given set of assets that indicates the balance of assets that may, under certain assumptions, achieve the best return for a given level of risk.

Eligible Children – Dependent minor children, including step-children and adopted children, of deceased Federal employees and retirees who are eligible for a monthly survivor benefit. Benefits to minor children stop when they reach age 18, marry, or die.

Employer-Sponsored Retirement Plan – A tax-favored retirement plan that is sponsored by an employer. Among the more common employer-sponsored retirement plans are 401(k) plans, 403(b) plans, simplified employee pension plans, and profit-sharing plans.

Equity – The value of a person's ownership in real property or securities; the market value of a property or business, less all claims and liens upon it.

ERISA – The Employee Retirement Income Security Act is a federal law covering all aspects of employee retirement plans. If employers provide plans, they must be adequately funded and provide for vesting, survivor's rights, and disclosures.

ESOP (Employee Stock Ownership Plan) – A defined contribution retirement plan in which company contributions must be invested primarily in qualifying employer securities.

Estate Conservation – Activities coordinated to provide for the orderly and cost-effective distribution of an individual's assets at the time of his or her death. Estate conservation often includes the use of wills and trusts.

Estate Tax – Upon the death of a decedent, federal and state governments impose taxes on the value of the estate left to others (with limitations).

Executor – A person named by the probate courts or the will to carry out the directions and requests of the decedent.

Executive Bonus Plan – The employer pays for a benefit that is owned by the executive. The bonus could take the form of cash, automobiles, life insurance, or other items of value to the executive.

The Federal Employees Retirement System – See *FERS*.

Fee-for-Service Plan – A traditional type of insurance that lets you use any doctor or hospital, but you usually must pay a deductible and coinsurance. These plans are called fee-for-service because doctors and other providers are paid for service, such as an office visit, or test. They help control costs by managing some aspects of patient cost. FEHB fee-for-service plans also provide access to preferred provider organizations (PPOs).

FEHB – The Federal Employees Health Benefits law or program.

FERS (The Federal Employees Retirement System) – The modern retirement plan established in 1986 and offered to all U.S. Government employees which combines Social Security benefits with an annual pension.

Fixed Annuity – An annuity contract that pays out a guaranteed fixed rate of interest. Fixed annuities are somewhat similar to Certificates of Deposit, except they grow tax-deferred and can be paid out in installments.

Fixed Income – Income from investments such as certificates of deposit, Social Security benefits, pension benefits, some annuities, or most bonds that is the same every month.

Fundamental Analysis – An approach to the stock market in which specific factors—such as the price-to-earnings ratio, yield, or return on equity—are used to determine which stocks may be favorable for investment in the current economic environment.

401(k) Plan – A defined contribution plan that may be established by a company for retirement. Employees may allocate a portion of their salaries into this plan, and contributions are excluded from their income for tax purposes (with limitations). Earnings will compound tax deferred.

403(b) Plan – A defined contribution plan that may be established by a non-profit organization or school for retirement. Employees may allocate a portion of their salaries into this plan, and contributions are excluded from their income for tax purposes (with limitations). Earnings will compound tax deferred.

Gift Taxes – A federal tax levied on the transfer of property as a gift. This tax is paid by the donor. The first $13,000 a year (indexed for inflation) from a donor to each recipient is exempt from tax. Most states also impose a gift tax.

Government Pension Offset (GPO) – A part of Social Security law that affects CSRS retirees who are also entitled to a Social Security spouse or survivor

benefit. It is sometimes referred to as the "Public Pension Offset." The Social Security benefit is reduced because the CSRS retiree is also receiving a pension from employment that was not covered by Social Security. If you elect FERS, you must be covered for 5 years to avoid the Government Pension Offset.

Health Maintenance Organization (HMO) – A type of health benefits plan that provides care through a network of doctors and hospitals in particular geographic or service areas. HMOs coordinate the health care services you receive. Your eligibility to enter an HMO is determined by where you live or, for some plans, where you work. Some FEHB HMOs have agreements with providers in other service areas for non-emergency care if you travel or are away for extended periods.

High-3 Average Salary – Your "high-3" average salary is determined by finding your highest average basic pay over any three year period. The three years must be consecutive. Generally, the final three years of service include the highest pay, but pay from an earlier period can be used if it was higher. More correctly called your "high-36-months" average salary.

Holographic Will –A will entirely in the handwriting of the testator. Without witnesses, holographic wills are valid and enforceable only in some states.

I-Bond – A type of U.S. Savings Bond designed to pay interest on an accrual basis at a rate that keeps up with inflation. They are issued at par and have 30 year maturities.

Immediate Annuity – An annuity that begins no later than one month after the date the insurance would otherwise stop. An annuity under 5 CFR 842.204(a)(1) for which the date has been postponed under 5 CFR 842.204.

Index – A calculation that uses a selection of stocks or bonds to gauge a certain market. The Dow Jones Industrial Average, for example, is an index of 30 large industrial companies on the New York Stock Exchange.

Individual Retirement Arrangement (IRA) – Contributions to a traditional IRA are deductible from earned income in the calculation of federal and state income taxes if the taxpayer meets certain requirements. Any earnings accumulate tax deferred until withdrawn, and withdrawals are taxed as ordinary income. A 10% penalty tax may apply to withdrawals prior to age 59½. Individuals not eligible to make deductible contributions may make nondeductible

contributions (the earnings on which would be tax deferred), or may contribute to a Roth IRA (income eligibility limits apply).

Inflation – An increase in the price of products and services over time. The government's main measure of inflation is the Consumer Price Index (CPI).

Inflationary Risk – The loss of purchasing power of an investment over time due to inflation.

Intestate – When a person dies without leaving a valid will. State law then determines who inherits the property or serves as guardian for any minor children.

Investment Class – A broad class of assets with similar characteristics. The seven investment classes include U.S. Stocks, U.S. Bonds, Foreign Bonds, Real Estate, Cash, Gold, and Natural Resources.

Irrevocable Trust – A trust that may not be modified or terminated by the trustor after its creation.

Joint and Survivor Annuity – Most pension plans must offer this form of pension plan payout that pays over the life of the retiree and his or her spouse after the retiree dies. The retiree and his or her spouse must specifically choose not to accept this payment form.

Jointly Held Property – Property owned by two or more persons under joint tenancy, tenancy in common, or, in some states, community property.

Joint Tenancy – Co-ownership of property by two or more people in which the survivor(s) automatically assumes ownership of a decedent's interest.

Keogh Plan – This retirement plan, named for Eugene Keogh, is designed for self-employed individuals. Self-employed income up to the contribution limit may be deducted from compensation and set aside into the plan.

Letter of Instruction – A document that can aid the executor of an estate in the settlement process by providing practical information such as contacts, the whereabouts of certain assets, and a plain English overview of the estate plan.

Liability – Any claim against the assets of a person or corporation: accounts payable, wages and salaries payable, dividends declared payable, accrued taxes payable, and fixed or long-term obligations such as mortgages, debentures, and bank loans.

Life Expectancy – The actuarial estimate of how long a person will live, based on demographic age and health data.

Limited Partnership – Limited partnerships pool the money of investors to develop or purchase income-producing properties. When the partnership subsequently receives income from these properties, it passes the income on to its investors as dividend payments.

Liquidity – The ease with which an asset or security can be converted into cash without loss of principal.

Liquidity Risk – The risk of not being able to access an investment when it is needed, or having to pay a penalty or fine in order to do so.

Lump-Sum Distribution – The disbursement of the entire value of a profit-sharing plan, pension plan, annuity, or similar account to the account owner or beneficiary. Lump sum distributions may be rolled over into another tax-deferred account.

Marginal Tax Bracket – The range of taxable income that is taxable at a certain rate. Currently, there are six marginal tax brackets; 10 percent, 15 percent, 25 percent, 28 percent, 33 percent, and 35 percent.

Marital Deduction – A provision of the tax code that allows all the assets of a decreased spouse to pass to the surviving spouse free from estate taxes. This provision is also referred to as the unlimited marital deduction.

Market Risk – The possibility that the value of an investment purchased may decline as a result of market conditions. All investments that are not guaranteed for principal are subject to this risk.

Medicare Managed Care Plan – A managed care plan such as an HMO or PPO that contracts with Medicare to enroll Medicare beneficiaries. Services must be obtained from the Managed Care Plan's network of doctors and hospitals to receive plan benefits. The Managed Care Plan may charge a monthly premium and require co-payments.

Minimum Retirement Age – This is the age at which you could have first retired had you not become disabled.

Municipal Bond – A debt security issued by municipalities. The income from municipal bonds is usually exempt from federal income taxes. In many states, it is also exempt from state income taxes.

Official Personnel Folder – Your personnel records that are maintained by your employing office.

Open Season – The annual time period set by OPM in which all eligible persons may elect or change their health benefits coverage.

Option A – $10,000 in coverage that you can elect in addition to Basic Insurance. Also called Standard Optional Insurance.

Option B – Life Insurance coverage equal to up to 5 multiples of your annual basic rate of pay that you can elect in addition to Basic Insurance. Also called Additional Optional Insurance.

Option C – Life Insurance coverage to insure your spouse and eligible child(ren), that you can elect in addition to Basic Insurance up to 5 multiples of the coverage amounts (each multiple equals $5,000 for a spouse and $2,500 for an eligible child). Also called Family Optional Insurance.

Panic – The feeling that inevitably overwhelms you when you come to the realization you will not have enough money to retire and have not prepared adequately for the last stage of your life.

Patriot Bonds – The name given to all Series EE Bonds issued after 9/11.

Preferred Provider Organization (PPO) – A fee-for-service option where you can choose plan-selected providers who have arrangements with them. When you use a PPO provider, you pay less money out-of-pocket for medical services than when you use a non-PPO provider.

Personal Financial Management Professional – A financial services professional who helps individuals coordinate their financial affairs to achieve their financial objectives.

Pooled Income Fund – A trust created by a charitable organization that combines the contributions of several donors and distributes income to those donors based on the earnings of the trust. The trust is managed by the charitable organization and contributions are partially deductible for income tax purposes.

Portfolio – All investments held by an individual or a mutual fund.

Post-65 Reduction in Insurance – The amount by which your insurance coverage reduces after your 65th birthday (or retirement, if later). For Basic Insurance, the choices are 75% Reduction, 50% Reduction, and No Reduction. For

Options B and C, the choices are Full Reduction and No Reduction. There is no choice for Option A; it reduces by 75%.

Preferred Stock – A class of stock with claim to a company's earnings before payment can be made on the common stock and usually entitled to priority over common stock if the company liquidates. Generally, preferred stocks pay dividends at a fixed rate.

Prenuptial Agreement – A legal agreement arranged before marriage stating who owns property acquired before marriage and during marriage and how property will be divided in the event of divorce. ERISA benefits are not affected by prenuptial agreements.

Price / Earnings Ratio (P/E Ratio) – The market price of a stock divided by the company's annual earnings per share. Since the P/E ratio is a widely regarded yardstick for investors, it often appears with stock price quotations.

Principal – In a security, the principal is the amount of money that is invested, excluding earnings. In a debt instrument such as a bond, it is the face amount.

Probate – The court-supervised process in which a decedent's estate is settled and distributed.

Profit-Sharing Plan – An agreement under which employees share in the profits of their employer. The company makes annual contributions to the employees' accounts. These funds usually accumulate tax deferred until the employee retires or leaves the company.

Prospectus – A document provided by investment companies to prospective investors. The prospectus gives information needed by investors to make informed decisions prior to investing. The prospectus includes information on the minimum investment amount, the investment objectives, past performance, risk level, sales charges, management fees, and any other expense information about the investment, as well as a description of the services provided to investors.

Qualified Domestic Relations Order (QDRO) – At the time of divorce, this order would be issued by a state domestic relations court and would require that an employee's ERISA retirement plan accrued benefits be divided between the employee and the spouse. QDRO orders do not apply to CSRS or FERS annuities. See Section 8345 (j) of title 5US6.

Qualified Retirement Plan – A pension, profit-sharing, or qualified savings plan that is established by an employer for the benefit of the employees. These plans must be established in conformity with IRS rules. Contributions accumulate tax deferred until withdrawn and are deductible to the employer as a current business expense.

Redeposit – A redeposit is the repayment of retirement deductions that were previously withheld and refunded to you, plus interest. You are not required to make this type of payment.

Reinvestment Risk – The risk that a fixed-income investment that matures may not be able to be reinvested at as good a rate as it was previously. This risk is present in declining interest rate environments.

Retirement Earnings Test – A calculation to estimate how much your Social Security benefits may be reduced if you continue to work after applying for benefits and before your full retirement age.

Risk – The chance that an investor will lose all or part of an investment.

Risk-Adverse – Refers to the assumption that rational investors will choose the security with the least risk if they can maintain the same return. As the level of risk goes up, so must the expected return on the investment.

Rollover – A method by which an individual can transfer the assets from one retirement program to another without the recognition of income for tax purposes. The requirements for a rollover depend on the type of program from which the distribution is made and the type of program receiving the distribution.

Roth IRA – A special type of IRA that offers tax-free accumulation and tax-free withdrawals if certain conditions are met. Contributions are non-deductible, and qualified distributions are not included in your gross income.

Security – Evidence of an investment, either in direct ownership (as with stocks), creditorship (as with bonds), or indirect ownership (as with options).

Simplified Employee Pension Plan (SEP) – A type of plan under which the employer contributes to an employee's IRA. Contributions may be made up to a certain limit and are immediately vested.

Single-Life Annuity – An insurance-based contract that provides future payments at regular intervals in exchange for current premiums. It is generally used as a supplement to retirement income and pays over the life of one individual, usually the retiree, with no rights of payment to any survivor.

Split-Dollar Plan – An arrangement under which two parties (usually a corporation and employee) share the cost of a life insurance policy and split the proceeds.

Spousal IRA – An IRA designed for a couple when one spouse has no earned income. The maximum combined contribution that can be made each year to an IRA and a spousal IRA is $5,000 (2010; indexed for inflation) or 100% of earned income, whichever is less.

Taxable Income – The amount of income used to compute tax liability. It is determined by subtracting adjustments, itemized deductions or the standard deduction, and personal exemptions from gross income.

Tax Bracket – The range of taxable income that is taxed at a certain rate. Brackets are expressed by their marginal tax rate.

Tax Credit – Tax credits, the most appealing type of tax deductions, are subtracted directly, dollar for dollar, from your income tax bill.

Tax Deferred – Interest, dividends, or capital gains that grow untaxed in certain accounts or plans until they are withdrawn.

Tax-Exempt Bonds – Under certain conditions, the interest from bonds issued by states, cities, and certain other government agencies is exempt from federal income taxes. In many states, the interest from tax-exempt bonds will also be exempt from state and local income taxes.

Technical Analysis – An approach to investing in stocks in which a stock's past performance is mapped onto charts. These charts are examined to find familiar patterns to use as an indicator of the stock's future performance.

Temporary Continuation of Coverage (TCC) – A provision of the FEHB law that allows Federal employees who separate from service and family members who lose eligibility to temporarily continue FEHB coverage.

Tenancy in Common – A form of co-ownership. Upon the death of a co-owner, his or her interest passes to his or her chosen beneficiaries and not to the surviving owner or owners.

Terminally Ill – For purposes of qualifying for a living benefit, having a medical prognosis of a life expectancy of nine months or less.

Term Insurance – Term life insurance provides a death benefit if the insured dies. Term insurance does not accumulate cash value and ends after a certain number of years or at a certain age.

Testator – One who has made a will or dies leaving a will.

Total Return – The total of all earnings from a given investment including dividends, interest, and any capital gain.

Trust – A legal entity created by an individual in which one person or institution holds the right to manage property or assets for the benefit of someone else. Types of trusts include:

- **Testamentary Trust** – A trust established by a will that takes effect upon death.

- **Living Trust** – A trust created by a person during his or her lifetime.

- **Revocable Trust** – A trust in which the creator reserves the right to modify or terminate the trust.

Thrift Savings Plan (TSP) – A defined contribution savings plan for eligible government employees administered by the Federal Retirement Thrift Investment Board.

Trustee – An individual or institution appointed to administer a trust for its beneficiaries.

Trustee-to-Trustee – A method of transferring retirement plan assets from one employer's plan to another employer's plan or to an IRA. One benefit of this method is that no federal income tax will be withheld by the trustee of the first plan.

Unified Credit – A credit that may be applied against an individual's gift or estate taxes. The unified credit will increase in upcoming years, and in 2009 will exempt an estate valued at $3.5 million from federal estate taxes.

Universal Life Insurance – A type of life insurance that combines a death benefit with a cash-value element that accumulates tax deferred at current interest rates. Under a universal life insurance policy, the policyholder can increase or decrease his or her coverage, with limitations, without purchasing a new policy.

Viatical Settlement Firm – A private company that exchanges cash for assignment of life insurance to a terminally or chronically ill person.

Volatility – The range of price swings of a security or market over time.

Welfare Benefit Plan – An employee benefit plan that provides such benefits as medical, sickness, accident, disability, death, or unemployment benefits.

Whole Life Insurance – A type of life insurance that offers a death benefit and also accumulates cash value, tax deferred, at fixed interest rates. Whole life insurance policies generally have a fixed annual premium that does not rise over the duration of the policy. Whole life insurance is also referred to as "ordinary" or "straight" life insurance.

Will – A legal document that declares a person's wishes concerning the disposition of property, the guardianship of his or her children, and the administration of the estate after his or her death.

Windfall Elimination Provision (WEP) – Reduces the amount of your Social Security benefits if you receive a pension based on work for an employer that did not withhold Social Security taxes from your salary.

Yield – In general, the yield is the amount of current income provided by an investment. For stocks, the yield is calculated by dividing the total of the annual dividends by the current price. For bonds, the yield is calculated by dividing the annual interest by the current price. The yield is distinguished from the return, which includes price appreciation or depreciation.

Zero-Coupon Bond – This type of bond makes no periodic interest payments but instead is sold at a steep discount from its face value. Bondholders receive the face value of their bonds when the bonds mature.

Index